HOUSING ISSUES, LAWS AND PROGRAMS

PUBLIC HOUSING: BACKGROUND AND ISSUES

HOUSING ISSUES, LAWS AND PROGRAMS

Additional books in this series can be found on Nova's website under the Series tab.

Additional E-books in this series can be found on Nova's website under the E-books tab.

HOUSING ISSUES, LAWS AND PROGRAMS

PUBLIC HOUSING: BACKGROUND AND ISSUES

SARA M. LARSEN
EDITOR

Nova Science Publishers, Inc.
New York

Library of Congress Cataloging-in-Publication Data

Public housing : background and issues / editor, Sara M. Larsen.
p. cm.
Includes index.
ISBN 978-1-61324-778-5 (hbk.)
1. Public housing--United States. 2. Low-income housing--United States. 3. Housing policy--United States. I. Larsen, Sara M.
HD7288.78.U5P83 2011
363.5'850973--dc23

2011017467

Published by Nova Science Publishers, Inc. † New York

CONTENTS

Preface		**vii**
Chapter 1	Introduction to Public Housing *Maggie McCarty*	**1**
Chapter 2	Public Housing: Fact Sheet on the Operating Fund Formula *Maggie McCarty*	**55**
Chapter 3	HOPE VI Public Housing Revitalization Program: Background, Funding, and Issues *Maggie McCarty*	**65**
Chapter 4	Community Service Requirement for Residents of Public Housing *Maggie McCarty*	**95**
Chapter 5	HUD's Oversight of Housing Agencies Should Focus More on Inappropriate Use of Program Funds *United States Government Accountability Office*	**103**
Index		**135**

PREFACE

The idea of a federal public housing program began taking shape in the 1930s during the Great Depression. Its purpose was intended to be twofold: the housing created would respond to a lack of sanitary housing available at a low cost to families who had fallen on hard times, and the construction of the housing would lead to the creation of jobs and economic growth. However, the idea of the federal government providing housing proved to be controversial. This book examines the history of the federal housing program; current policy issues; how it is administered and funded and the characteristics of public housing properties and the households they serve.

Chapter 1- "Public housing" is often used as a generic term to refer to all publicly assisted housing, but the term "public housing" actually refers to a specific federal program. Created in 1937, the low-rent public housing program was the first major federal rental housing assistance program. The program initially subsidized the construction, and later the ongoing operation and maintenance, of multifamily rental housing properties for low-income families. While public housing is a federally created and funded program, the properties are owned and managed at the local level by quasi-governmental public housing authorities (PHAs) under contract with the federal government. Given this unique federal-local relationship, the program is governed in part by federal rules and regulations and in part by policies set at the local level.

Chapter 2- The local public housing authorities (PHAs) that administer the federal public housing program began receiving their annual federal operating subsidies under a new formula in January 2007. As a result of this formula change, some PHAs were eligible for an increase in their eligibility for funding and others were eligible for a decrease. Both the increases and the decreases were phased in (over two and five years, respectively) and PHAs that faced declines were eligible to limit their losses by adopting management reforms—which were also a part of the new operating fund requirements—earlier than required.

Since the formula is only used to determine eligibility for funding, the amount that a PHA qualifies for under the formula (whether it is an increase or a decrease) will be reduced if Congress appropriates less money than is necessary to fund all agencies at 100% of their eligibility, which it has done in the past.

Chapter 3- The Revitalization of Distressed Public Housing program, referred to as HOPE VI, has been credited with eliminating and replacing some of the most dangerous and dilapidated public housing in the country with new mixed income communities. However, the program has come under scrutiny for slow expenditure of funds and for displacing poor families. Reflecting these criticisms, the Bush Administration requested no new funding for the program in each budget request from FY2004-FY2009, and the Obama Administration requested no new funding (proposing, instead, that Congress fund a new program) in the FY2010 and FY2011 budget requests. Congress responded by continuing to fund the program, but at less than a quarter of what it had been funded at in FY2003 and prior years.

Chapter 4- The Quality Housing and Work Responsibility Act of 1998 (P.L. 105-276) included provisions designed to promote employment and self-sufficiency among residents of assisted housing, including a mandatory work or community service requirement for residents of public housing. Non-elderly, non-disabled, non-working residents of public housing are required to participate in eight hours per month of either community service or economic self-sufficiency activities in order to maintain their eligibility for public housing. This provision was briefly implemented in FY2001; however, an act of Congress suspended enforcement of the provision in FY2002. That suspension ended in 2003 and residents of public housing are once again required to comply with the community service requirement.

Chapter 5- The Department of Housing and Urban Development (HUD) provided over $6.7 billion in fiscal year 2008 to housing agencies to operate, modernize, and develop about 1.2 million public housing units. It is important that HUD exercise sufficient oversight of housing agencies to help ensure that public housing funds are being used as intended and properly managed. In this report, GAO examines HUD's oversight processes for detecting housing agencies at risk of inappropriate use and mismanagement of public housing funds. GAO analyzed HUD financial data on about 3,300 housing agencies, compared HUD's oversight policies with program and agency objectives, and interviewed agency officials.

In: Public Housing: Background and Issues ISBN: 978-1-61324-778-5
Editor: Sara M. Larsen

Chapter 1

INTRODUCTION TO PUBLIC HOUSING*

Maggie McCarty

SUMMARY

"Public housing" is often used as a generic term to refer to all publicly assisted housing, but the term "public housing" actually refers to a specific federal program. Created in 1937, the low-rent public housing program was the first major federal rental housing assistance program. The program initially subsidized the construction, and later the ongoing operation and maintenance, of multifamily rental housing properties for low-income families. While public housing is a federally created and funded program, the properties are owned and managed at the local level by quasi-governmental public housing authorities (PHAs) under contract with the federal government. Given this unique federal-local relationship, the program is governed in part by federal rules and regulations and in part by policies set at the local level.

The public housing program serves some of the poorest families in the nation, including persons who are elderly, persons who are living with disabilities, and other families with and without children. Families who live in public housing generally pay rent equal to 30% of their adjusted gross income; average rents paid by public housing families lag substantially behind private market rents paid by similar families.

* This is an edited, reformatted and augmented version of a Congressional Research Service publication, CRS Report for Congress R41654, from www.crs.gov, dated February 24, 2011.

Public housing properties themselves can be high-rise buildings, low-rise buildings, scattered site properties, and even part of mixed-income housing developments. Construction and acquisition of new public housing units effectively ended after the federal government stopped funding new development in the mid-1990s, although they began significantly decreasing much earlier as other models of providing housing assistance grew in popularity. As public housing properties have fallen into disrepair and been demolished, the number of public housing units has begun to decrease. Today, there are roughly 1.2 million units under contract and receiving federal funding, down from over 1.4 million units at the program's peak. Federal funding comes from two main formula grants—the Public Housing Capital Fund and the Public Housing Operating Fund— which are meant to supplement the rents collected by PHAs to meet the operation, maintenance, and capital needs of public housing. There have also been several competitive grant programs that provide additional funding to PHAs, including the HOPE VI program. In recent years, regular annual appropriations for public housing have generally been in the range of $6 billion to $7 billion per year, with an additional $4 billion provided by the 2009 economic stimulus legislation.

In response to concerns about the adequacy of federal funding levels—paired with federal restrictions on tenant rents—to meet the capital needs of public housing, proposals have been introduced to promote private investment in public housing in order to preserve the existing stock. An increasing number of PHAs have pursued private financing to meet their capital needs in recent years. However, recent proposals calling for an expansion in the role of private finance in public housing have been met with concerns about the potential for the "privatization" of public housing and a loss of affordability. As the program continues to decline in terms of the number of families it serves, questions are arising about the role the program plays, and should play in the future, in terms of federal housing policy.

This report is meant to serve as an introduction to the federal public housing program. It provides information on the history of the program, how it is administered and funded, and the characteristics of public housing properties and the households they serve. While it introduces current policy issues, a full analysis of those issues and discussion of current legislation is not included in this report.

INTRODUCTION

Housing is primarily a private market enterprise in the United States. Most housing in this country is privately built and owned and most regulation of that process is done at the state and local level. However, the federal government has played a role for many years in assisting in the provision of safe, decent, and affordable housing for families of modest means. The low-rent public housing program was the original effort through which the federal government supported this policy goal. While public housing is a federally created and funded program, administered at the federal level by the Department of Housing and Urban Development (HUD), the properties are owned and managed at the local level by quasi-governmental public housing authorities (PHAs) under contract with the federal government. Given this unique federal-local relationship, the program is governed in part by federal rules and regulations and in part by policies set at the local level.

The program was controversial from the start, with opponents contending that it subverted local control and interfered with private enterprise. Later, criticism grew about the conditions of the housing the program provided. Concern was expressed about the quality of life public housing provided to the families it served, as well as the character of the tenants the program served and the effect public housing was having on the communities in which it was located. Over time, in response to these critiques and others, the public housing model—publicly owned and subsidized apartment buildings for poor families—was replaced with other models of assistance. While no new public housing is authorized to be funded and built, much of the existing stock of public housing built under the original program remains.

Today's roughly 1.2 million units of public housing are home to some of the poorest families in the nation, including persons who are elderly, persons living with disabilities, and other families with and without children. In some cases, these families live in high-quality housing in neighborhoods of opportunity; in other cases, these families live in housing that is physically decrepit, socially isolated, and plagued by social ills. The federal government currently pays roughly $6 billion to $7 billion per year to support the remaining stock of public housing and there are differences of opinion about whether this program is a worthwhile federal investment or whether recent funding levels reflect an inadequate federal investment.

This report is meant to serve as an introduction to the federal public housing program. It provides information on the history of the program, how it is administered and funded, and the characteristics of public housing properties and the households they serve. While it introduces current policy issues, a full analysis of those issues and discussion of current legislation is not included in this report.

BRIEF HISTORY OF THE PUBLIC HOUSING PROGRAM

In order to understand today's public housing program, and the issues surrounding the program, it is useful to know the background of how it evolved. The following section of this report provides a short history of the public housing program. It should not be considered a comprehensive or exhaustive treatment of the topic.

The Housing Act of 1937: The Beginning of Public Housing

The idea of a federal public housing program began taking shape in the 1930s during the Great Depression. Its purpose was intended to be twofold: the housing created would respond to a lack of sanitary housing available at a low cost to families who had fallen on hard times, and the construction of the housing would lead to the creation of jobs and economic growth.[1] However, the idea of the federal government providing housing proved to be controversial. Opponents saw government involvement in housing as a step towards socialism, the building industries thought that they could handle the nation's housing problems without government intervention, and some local governments were concerned that federal housing would encroach on their sovereignty.[2]

The Housing Act of 1937 (P.L. 75-412) attempted to balance some of these concerns in the way that it designed the low-rent public housing program. Under the terms of the act, public housing properties would be built and owned only by state-chartered and locally governed public housing authorities (PHAs). This gave states and localities the right to choose whether or not to participate in the program by deciding whether or not to create PHAs. The federal government would provide capital financing under long-term Annual Contributions Contracts (ACCs). These contracts would spell out the federal requirements of the program; however, many of the decisions about how the housing was designed, where it was located, and who could live in it would be left to the PHAs. Public housing's operations would be sustained primarily on tenant rents, which meant that families would be required to have incomes high enough to pay the rents charged for public housing units. However, in part to prevent competition with the private market, the authorizing statute dictated that families who wanted to live in public housing could not have incomes that exceeded five times the rents (six times in the case of large families). Further, the law required that for each new unit of housing built, an unsafe or unsanitary unit had to be eliminated (a concept often referred to as "slum clearance").[3]

Not long after the program was created, World War II shifted the focus of federal involvement in housing. The Lanham Act of 1940 halted new development under the low-rent public housing program in favor of government construction of housing for war workers.[4] The act also gave war workers priority for existing public housing units.[5] By the end of the 1940s, around 200,000 public housing units had been built and were under contract.[6]

The earliest residents of public housing were primarily working class families who were "temporarily poor" because of the Depression. Later, many war workers moved into public housing. As the nation began to prosper again, many families in public housing had income above what was considered to be low income.[7]

The Housing Act of 1949: Expansion and Ties to Urban Renewal

After being diverted to support the war effort, the low-rent public housing program was restarted at the end of the decade by the Housing Act of 1949 (P.L. 81-171). That act created a federal policy goal of "a decent home and suitable living environment for every American family." It authorized the Urban Renewal program—formalizing the policy of slum clearance evident in the 1937 act—and required communities to give preference for public housing units to families displaced by Urban Renewal. The act expanded the authorization for new public housing units, calling for the creation of 810,000 units by 1954 (or 135,000 units per year). At the same time, the act added new requirements. Out of concern about crowding out private market housing, the act instituted construction cost limits and added a requirement that public housing rents be at least 20% below prevailing market rents for safe and decent housing. Given that upper income eligibility limits were tied to rents (i.e., incomes could not exceed five times the rents), this meant that income eligibility limits would be lowered. Additionally, the act required that the Annual Contributions Contracts be amended to require the eviction of tenants whose income exceeded the limits.[8]

While the 1949 act restarted the public housing program, its goal of 810,000 units in six years was not met. The year after the enactment of the 1949 act, President Truman lowered the rate of construction to roughly half the authorized level in response to concerns about materials shortages resulting from the outbreak of hostilities in Korea.[9] Congress followed suit by further lowering the authorized annual level of public housing construction starts each year in the appropriations acts.[10] Also, opposition from local communities made it difficult for some PHAs to get approval to build public housing.[11] As a result, fewer units were built in the 1950s than were envisioned by the 1949 act. By the end of 1957, only about 210,000 of the 810,000 units authorized by the 1949 act were under management.[12]

The characteristics of the tenants served in public housing also began changing during this period. The policy changes included in the 1949 act, taken together, would mean that public housing would serve families with income lower than what was originally required under the 1937 act. This change in the income character of tenants is evident in the fact that from 1952 to 1962, the number of families in public housing receiving income from private or public assistance programs rose from 29% to 46%. Further, given that public housing development was explicitly tied to Urban Renewal after 1949, the program began to house more families of color, particularly black families, who had been uprooted and displaced by Urban Renewal. From the beginning of the 1950s to the end, the percentage of nonwhite families living in public housing increased from 36% to 46%.[13] In an era of legal segregation and discrimination, the increasing proportion of black families living in public housing led to great opposition to new public housing development in some predominantly white communities and to the perpetuation of segregation in public housing properties themselves.

1960s: New Forms of Assistance and the End of Legal Discrimination

The 1960s brought a new vision with regard to federal housing assistance. Several new programs were developed to subsidize privately owned rental properties, as opposed to publicly owned properties, including the Section 236 rent supplement program serving low-income families and seniors; the Section 202 program serving the elderly; and the Section 221d(3) program serving families with incomes too high for public housing but too low to afford housing in the private market.[14] Another program, the Section 23 leased housing program, was a new public housing program designed to utilize private market units. It permitted PHAs to lease private market units on behalf of public housing-eligible families. Also, by the late 1960s the Turnkey model of public housing began growing in popularity; under the Turnkey approach, a private developer builds housing on land he owns and then sells the property to a PHA to use as public housing.[15] These new models of assistance, because they utilized private market participants, were thought to be more efficient and timely. Despite the introduction of new programs, the number of public housing units increased significantly during the 1960s to over 800,000 units, an increase from about half a million units at the beginning of the decade.[16]

The 1960s brought other important changes for public housing related to the social aspects of the program. A Presidential Order, Supreme Court cases, and civil rights legislation worked to make it illegal to deny public housing assistance to families based on their race and to systematically segregate public housing residents by race, which had been common since the inception of the program.[17] While such discriminatory actions were officially outlawed during this period, desegregation and changes in community attitudes towards integrated public housing were not immediate and courts had to intervene.[18] Out of concern about the ramifications of concentrations of poverty, the Housing and Urban Development Act of 1968 prohibited the construction of new high-rise public housing projects for families.[19]

The Housing and Urban Development Act of 1969 made a fundamental change to the rent structure in public housing; the Brooke Amendment capped tenant contributions toward rent at 25% of family income.[20] This change was made out of concern that rents charged for public housing were becoming too high for poor families to afford. To help meet the operating needs of public housing, the 1969 act also authorized HUD to begin providing operating assistance to PHAs, in addition to capital funding to cover the costs of the bonds they had issued to build public housing.[21]

Over this period, the income character of the tenants in public housing had also continued to change. Policy changes (such as the limit on the number of over-income families who could live in public housing, reductions in income eligibility standards, and preferences for families displaced by urban renewal) partnered with market changes (such as the post-war housing boom, increasing rates of homeownership, and suburbanization) resulted in public housing serving the poorest tenants, many of whom were receiving other public assistance.[22] Until passage of the Brooke Amendment, the rents these very poor families paid were, in many cases, higher than what might be considered "affordable" to them, but not high enough to provide sufficient income to allow PHAs to properly maintain public housing properties. Although Congress eventually began providing additional operating subsidies to public housing after passage of the Brooke Amendment, some public housing developments, facing inadequate rental income and insufficient federal subsidies to maintain their properties, fell into severe disrepair. These realities—poorer tenants paying lower rents, insufficient operating income, and deteriorating units—shaped the public housing debates of the decade to follow.

The 1970s and the Rise of Section 8

By the early 1970s, construction programs were subject to growing criticism for taking too long to develop and being too expensive. The Housing and Urban Development Act of 1970 required that at least 30% of new public housing units be created through the Section 23 leased housing program, which utilized the existing housing stock rather than new construction.[23] The act also authorized a demonstration, called the Experimental Housing Allowance Program, to test the feasibility and effectiveness of giving families housing allowances in lieu of subsidized units. In 1973, President Nixon imposed a moratorium on all new housing construction commitments,[24] including those under public housing. He argued that the existing programs needed revisiting because they did not provide decent housing to families and cost the federal government too much to build and maintain.[25]

The Nixon Moratorium was ended as Congress authorized funding for new units of public housing and created new housing assistance programs.[26] The Housing and Community Development Act of 1974 created the Section 8 program, which continued the shift to subsidizing privately owned housing by pairing rental subsidies with private market housing units.[27] The Section 8 program was designed to respond to the criticisms of the earlier programs by including subsidies for private units and relying less heavily on new construction.

After the moratorium, the focus of federal housing assistance policy had shifted away from constructing new public housing units to new models using the existing and private housing market through the Section 8 program. Public housing averaged fewer than 37,000 reservations[28] for new units of public housing per year between 1975 and 1979, compared to an average of more than 275,000 reservations for new Section 8 assisted units per year over the same period.[29]

The 1980s: Withdrawing Further from Public Housing

The Omnibus Budget Reconciliation Act of 1981 made several significant changes to public housing.[30] It raised tenant rent contributions toward rent (as established by the Brooke Amendment at 25% of family income) to 30% of family income. Estimating that increased rents would decrease the need for federal operating subsidies, the act limited increases in funding for operating subsidies. At the same time, the act more deeply targeted assistance to the poorest families. Eligibility was largely[31] restricted to families with incomes below 50% of the local area median income and federal preferences were set to target assistance to the households assumed to have the greatest need, including those who were homeless, those who were severely cost burdened, and those living in substandard housing.[32]

The trend away from public housing continued with the Urban-Rural Recovery Act of 1983, which limited new construction of public housing to instances in which it would be less than the cost of acquiring existing housing.[33] At the same time, the act limited the ability of PHAs to demolish or dispose of public housing to cases where the unit could not be reasonably rehabilitated or the demolition/disposition would result in the acquisition of new housing. The 1983 act also authorized a demonstration testing a new form of Section 8 assistance, a portable voucher with more flexible standards. The voucher program was made permanent in 1988[34] and fully replaced the original Section 8 program.[35] The Housing and Community Development Act of 1987 further limited new public housing construction to only those cases where the PHA could certify that family housing demand could not be met through Section 8.[36] New public housing starts dropped off significantly during the 1980s in favor of the new Section 8 program.[37]

During the 1980s, concern continued to grow about the state of the existing public housing stock—both the physical soundness as well as the social health of public housing communities. In 1989, Congress established a National Commission on Severely Distressed Public Housing.[38] The commission was mandated to identify those public housing projects that were in a severe state of distress; assess the most promising strategies for improvement; and develop a national action plan. In 1992, the commission issued its findings and recommendations on the state of the nation's public housing. It reported finding residents living in fear of crime, high unemployment and limited opportunities for employment, insufficient resources to address the needs of residents, disincentives to self-sufficiency, and housing that had deteriorated to the point that it was physically dangerous.

The commission issued a wide range of recommendations, including increased social services for residents, increased funding for public housing capital needs, better performance assessment for PHAs, and experimentation with new forms of public-private partnerships. The commission labeled 6% of the public housing stock as severely distressed; at the time, this equaled 86,000 units.

1990s to Present: The End of Public Housing Development and Decline in Units

The National Affordable Housing Act of 1990[39] reacted to some of the concerns about public housing echoed by the National Commission. It authorized the Family Self Sufficiency program, designed to provide incentives for assisted families to increase their employment. It also required HUD to establish a formal PHA management assessment system, including mechanisms for intervening in cases of troubled housing authorities, and it established a new source of safety and security funding, the Drug Elimination Grant program. Shortly thereafter, the Housing and Community Development Act of 1992 created the Revitalization of Severely Distressed Public Housing program—commonly referred to as HOPE VI—which authorized HUD to make competitive grants to PHAs to undertake major redevelopment of distressed public housing.[40]

In 1995, the Clinton Administration proposed the "Reinvention Blueprint," which called for most public housing developments to be converted to vouchers.[41] At the same time, some Members of Congress were calling for the abolition of HUD.[42] While the Blueprint was not fully undertaken and HUD was not abolished, reform proposals, many of which were included in the Blueprint, were considered throughout the 1990s.

These efforts culminated with the passage of a major reform bill in 1998, the Quality Housing and Work Opportunity Reconciliation Act of 1998 (QHWRA; P.L. 105-276). QHWRA included provisions designed to promote local control, including the elimination of federal preferences. It established a requirement that PHAs develop annual and five-year plans detailing how they were using their local discretion. It gave PHAs the authority to convert their public housing properties to vouchers, and in some cases, required that conversion if it proved cost effective. Influenced by the welfare reform debates of the mid-1990s that were focused on promoting work,[43] QHWRA established a requirement that non-elderly, non-disabled residents be working or participating in community service or self-sufficiency activities for eight hours per month and created a disregard of newly earned income for some families. The act included authority for PHAs to leverage their public housing properties and funding in order to secure private resources (loans) for redevelopment. It also required HUD to develop a new formula for distributing operating funding to PHAs. Importantly, the act prohibited PHAs from using any federal capital or operating funding to develop net new public housing units.[44] While Congress had not provided funding for the development of new public housing units since FY1994,[45] this provision of QHWRA effectively prohibited any net new development,[46] even if funds were available.

More than a decade after enactment of QHWRA, the number of public housing units nationally has declined steadily, as more units are torn down than are rebuilt (see Figure 1). The HOPE VI program, which had become at least partly responsible for declines in the number of units, has had its funding reduced substantially, in part in reaction to concerns about slow spending, and in part in reaction to concerns about displaced residents. With the exception of an infusion of funding from the economic stimulus legislation in 2009,[47] capital funding has remained relatively level, despite a backlog in unmet capital needs. While PHAs have begun leveraging their public funds to raise private capital, the potential for leveraging sufficient funds to meet the full backlog of needs is limited. Given the reality of declining units, questions remain about the future of the public housing stock and the program's role in the future of federal housing assistance.

OVERVIEW OF THE PROGRAM

The following section of this report provides basic information about today's public housing program. It begins with a discussion of the unique administrative structure of the program, followed by a discussion of the program's policies and rules as they apply to public housing residents. For a more detailed description of program policies, see the program regulations at 24 C.F.R. Parts 901-972 and in the Public Housing Occupancy Guidebook.[48]

Administration

Public housing has a unique administrative structure that pairs local administration and local discretion with federal funding and federal regulations. Public housing properties are owned and managed by quasi-governmental local public housing authorities (PHAs). PHAs have contracts, called Annual Contributions Contracts (ACCs), with the federal government. Under the terms of their contracts, PHAs agree to administer their properties according to federal rules and regulations, and in exchange they receive federal funding in the form of operating and capital grants (discussed later in this report under "Funding"). These federal rules and regulations provide PHAs with more discretion in developing some policies (such as the admissions process), but less discretion in developing other policies (such as the income determination process). In areas where PHAs do have discretion to set local policies, they are required to develop those policies through a public process that allows for—and responds to—community feedback.

PHAs

PHAs were, for the most part, created by states in response to the federal government's creation of the low-rent public housing program. Their authorities and structures are dictated by the state laws under which they were chartered. PHAs typically have an executive director as well as a governing board. The board generally has members appointed by local government officials, but it may also have elected members. The board's role is generally to approve policy, clarify goals, and delegate responsibility and authority to the executive director, who acts on its behalf. While PHAs' governing structures are dictated primarily by their state charters, federal law mandates that, unless otherwise exempted, PHA boards must include at least one resident.[49]

While PHAs were created for the purpose of administering the federal low-rent public housing program, their missions have expanded over the years. Some PHAs administer state and local housing programs[50] and act as affordable housing developers in their communities. PHAs are also responsible for administering the federal Section 8 Housing Choice Voucher program;[51] in fact, some PHAs no longer administer public housing and only administer the voucher program.

Today, there are over 3,000 PHAs and they vary in size from the very small to the very large. Table 1 provides a breakdown of PHAs that administer public housing by size. The vast majority of PHAs–74% of all PHAs—are small (administering fewer than 250 units), but small PHAs only administer about 17% of all public housing units nationally. Over half of all units are administered by large PHAs (1250+ units). One PHA, the New York City Housing Authority (NYCHA) is noticeably larger than most other PHAs and accounts for over 13% of all public housing units nationwide.

Table 1. PHAs, by Size

Categories of Size	Number of PHAs	Percentage of PHAs	% of Units
NYCHA	1	0%	13%
1250+ units	133	4%	42%
500-1249 units	229	7%	15%
250-400 units	430	14%	13%
100-249 units	854	27%	11%
Less than 100 units	1,478	47%	6%
Total	3,125	100%	100%

Source: HUD CY2009 Operating Fund Report.

Part of the reason there are so many small PHAs is the way they were created by states; they were typically tied to a specific locality, such as a county or unit of local government. In recent years, there has been an increase in the number of smaller PHAs that have merged or formed consortia. In some cases, these mergers or consortia are designed to allow the agencies' programs— particularly the Section 8 voucher program—to be administered across a metropolitan region that crosses jurisdictional boundaries. In other cases, these mergers and consortia are meant to reduce administrative costs—for example, by requiring only one executive director for the consortia instead of one for each PHA—and to achieve efficiencies of scale. Academic researchers,[52] as well as the Bush[53] and Obama administrations,[54] have encouraged further PHA consolidation.

However, PHA consolidation can lead to a loss of local control for municipalities, and may therefore be unpopular with local leaders.

PHA Plans

As a condition of receiving federal funds, PHAs agree to administer their low-rent public housing properties according to federal rules and regulations. However, those rules and regulations give PHAs the discretion to develop their own local policies and procedures in many aspects of the program. Those local policies and procedures must be included in the PHAs' plans.

PHA plans are meant to provide information about how PHAs administer both their public housing and voucher programs as well as their intentions for the future. For anyone interested in a particular PHA's intentions, goals, and policies, the PHA plans can be a valuable resource. According to HUD's regulations:

> The purpose of the plans is to provide a framework for local accountability and an easily identifiable source by which public housing residents, participants in the tenant-based assistance program, and other members of the public may locate basic PHA policies, rules and requirements concerning the PHA's operations, programs and services. (24 C.F.R. 903.3)

PHAs are required to establish two plans: the five-year plan and the annual plan. Both plans must be developed with resident input and public participation, and the plans are subject to HUD approval. The five-year plan describes the PHA's mission, goals, and objectives and the PHA's progress towards meeting those goals and objectives. The goals and objectives are generally related to both the agency's physical housing stock as well as the agency's role in meeting the housing needs of lower-income families in their communities. The annual plan describes the PHA's day-to-day operations and policies. The policies and procedures spelled-out in the annual plan are expected to be consistent with the goals and objectives outlined in the five-year plan. Specifically, the annual plan must include information regarding, among other things,

- housing needs in the PHA's community;
- the PHA's policies that govern eligibility, selection, and admissions (as described in the agency's Admissions and Continued Occupancy Plan);
- the PHA's financial resources, as well as its most recent audit;
- the PHA's rent determination policies;
- the PHA's operation and management, including rules, standards, and policies that govern maintenance and management of housing owned, assisted, or operated by the PHA;
- the extent of capital improvement needs at the PHA's properties;
- any public housing developments designated as housing for the elderly or disabled;

- any plans to demolish or dispose of public housing, or convert any public housing to vouchers;
- the PHA's community service and self-sufficiency programs; and
- the PHA's safety and crime prevention measures. (24 C.F.R. 903.7)

PHAs are also required to establish Resident Advisory Boards to provide input in the planning process. Members of the Resident Advisory Boards are elected and are public housing residents and, if applicable, voucher holders. PHAs are required to consider Resident Advisory Board recommendations while they are developing their annual and five-year plans.[55]

In addition to soliciting input from residents, PHAs are required to solicit broader community input on their PHA plans. Specifically, PHAs are required to make their draft plans publicly available and hold public hearings on their content. The PHA plan cannot be formally adopted until the public hearing has been completed, the recommendations have been considered, and any changes have been made.[56]

PHAs submit their plans to HUD and they are subject to HUD's approval. HUD reviews the plans to ensure that they are complete, consistent with any other local HUD plans,[57] and consistent with federal law.[58]

Some PHAs are exempted from the annual and/or five-year planning process, and some are eligible for a streamlined annual plan process. Specifically, high performing PHAs, small PHAs (250 or fewer units), and Section 8 voucher-only PHAs are eligible to submit streamlined annual plans. Streamlined plans are not required to contain as much information as full plans, although PHAs must still give notice of how interested parties can obtain the information not contained in the streamlined annual plan. The Housing and Economic Recovery Act of 2008 (P.L. 110-289) included a title that exempted PHAs that administer 550 or fewer combined public housing units and Section 8 vouchers from filing an annual plan. PHAs that are considered troubled are not eligible for this exemption.[59]

PHAs participating in the Moving to Work Demonstration (MTW) may also be exempted from the standard annual and five-year plan requirements, although they are required to submit alternate annual MTW plans. (For an expanded discussion, see "Moving to Work" later in this report.)

Resident Involvement

According to HUD regulations, "residents shall be involved and participate in the overall policy development and direction of public housing operations."[60] There are several ways in which resident participation in the government and management of public housing is promoted or required. As noted already, most PHAs are required to have at least one resident on their governing boards and PHAs must establish Resident Advisory Boards to provide input in the PHA planning process.

Additionally, public housing residents have the right to organize and elect a resident council to represent their interests.[61] Most PHAs are required to set aside funding for resident participation activities, at least some of which is to be provided specifically for resident councils.[62] PHAs are required to recognize resident councils, and resident councils may provide input in all areas of PHA operations, including but not limited to occupancy, general management, maintenance, security, resident training, resident employment, social services, and modernization priorities.

Taking resident participation one step further, public housing residents may form resident management corporations, which are resident-sponsored entities that may enter into contracts with PHAs to undertake some or all of the management activities at a property (or properties). HUD's regulations state that HUD

> encourages [P]HAs, resident councils and resident management corporations to explore the various functions involved in management to identify appropriate opportunities for contracting with a resident management corporation. Potential benefits of resident-managed entities include improved quality of life, experiencing the dignity of meaningful work, enabling residents to choose where they want to live, and meaningful participation in the management of the housing development. (24 C.F.R. 964.15)

Public Housing Assessment System

HUD annually assesses the performance of the local PHAs that are administering the public housing and Section 8 Housing Choice Voucher programs. The current assessment of public housing program administration is called the Public Housing Assessment System (PHAS). PHAS includes reviews of indicators pertaining to the physical condition of an agency's housing stock, the financial condition of the agency, the agency's management performance, and the results of a survey of residents' satisfaction.[63]

PHAs that score 90% or better overall, and above 60% on all individual indicators, are considered high performers. High performers are eligible for reduced federal oversight (including a streamlined annual plan) and may be eligible for bonus funding.[64]

PHAs that score less than 60% overall, or on two or more of the PHAS indicators, are considered "troubled." Once a PHA is designated as troubled, the Secretary must notify the PHA of its status.[65] At the outset of a PHA's designation as troubled, it must develop a plan for its improvement with HUD.[66] In addition to helping agencies develop these plans, HUD has a number of options for aiding troubled agencies.[67] HUD can appoint a recovery team to help develop remedies, provide technical assistance and training, impose financial sanctions, or develop flexible arrangements with agencies tailored to their specific conditions.[68]

If a troubled PHA fails to make adequate progress, it may be found to be in substantial default of its Annual Contributions Contract (ACC)[69] with HUD.[70] A PHA can be found to be in substantial default for violations of the Fair Housing Act (including maintaining segregated public housing), physical deterioration of the public housing stock, management difficulties (ranging from unwillingness or inability to follow HUD's program rules to fraud), or any combination of these factors.

One of the options available to HUD is to place a troubled PHA that is found to be in substantial default in a receivership. Under a receivership, a PHA is stripped of all or part of its authority and that authority is granted to another party, referred to as a receiver. Under an administrative receivership,[71] HUD can either serve as the receiver itself and take temporary possession of all or part of the PHA, or the HUD can select another PHA or private housing management corporation to serve as the receiver and manage all or part of the PHA.[72]

According to HUD data from 2010, 50% of PHAs administering public housing were considered high performers, 44% were considered standard performers, 3% were considered substandard for financial reasons, 1% were considered substandard for physical reasons, and 1% were considered troubled (with an overall score of less than 60 or substandard scores on at least two indicators).[73]

Demolition, Disposition, and Conversion

As noted earlier, PHAs have contracts with the federal government governing their public housing properties. Under the terms of those contracts, PHAs must receive HUD's permission to make changes to their public housing stock. Specifically, PHAs must receive HUD's permission to either demolish or dispose of (sell) public housing units that are under contract.[74] Demolition and disposition of public housing is governed by Section 18 of the U.S. Housing Act.

In order for a demolition to be approved, the property must be found to be "obsolete as to physical condition, location, or other factors, making it unsuitable for housing purposes, and no reasonable program of modifications is cost-effective to return the public housing project or portion of the project to useful life."[75]

The criteria for approving a disposition are broader, but PHAs face restrictions on how they can use the proceeds from a disposition. In order for a disposition to be approved, the property must meet the following criteria:

> (a) Conditions in the area surrounding the project (density, or industrial or commercial development) adversely affect the health or safety of the tenants or the feasible operation of the project by the PHA; (b) Disposition allows the acquisition, development, or rehabilitation of other properties that will be more efficiently or effectively operated as low-income housing developments; (c) The PHA has otherwise determined the disposition to be appropriate for reasons that are consistent with the goals of the PHA and the PHA Plan and that are otherwise consistent with the Act. (24 C.F.R. 970.17)

However, the use of the proceeds from a disposition are limited. Unless waived by HUD, the proceeds must be used for the retirement of outstanding obligations. Any remaining proceeds must be used to provide low-income housing, or used for the benefit of the PHA's residents or to secure on-site commercial enterprises that are appropriate to serve the needs of the residents.[76]

If a public housing unit is demolished or disposed of, any displaced tenants must be provided with relocation assistance,[77] including comparable replacement housing. Replacement housing is generally provided in the form of either a residence in another public housing unit or a replacement voucher, referred to as a tenant protection voucher, which tenants can use to find housing in the private market.[78]

In addition to demolition and disposition, another way in which properties can leave the public housing stock is through conversion to vouchers. In 1996, Congress enacted a requirement that any property with more than 300 units and a vacancy rate of over 10% be assessed to determine its viability. This was referred to as the Section 202 mandatory conversion requirement.[79] If the assessment determined that it would cost more to rehabilitate the property than to provide residents with vouchers, then the property was to be removed from the public housing inventory in five years. The Quality Housing and Work Opportunity Act of 1998 (QHWRA; P.L. 105-276) rewrote and reinforced the mandatory conversion requirement (renaming it "required conversion") and added a voluntary conversion policy. Specifically, under QHWRA PHAs are required to assess for conversion all of their developments with 250 or more units and low occupancy. Covered developments must be converted to vouchers if the cost of modernizing them and operating them as public housing exceeds the cost of providing tenant-based vouchers. PHAs may choose to *voluntarily* convert developments in cases where it would (1) be beneficial to the residents, (2) be beneficial to the surrounding area, and (3) not have an adverse effect on the availability of affordable housing in the area. Voluntary conversions must also be cost-effective.

Since 2006, PHAs have been required to review their inventory annually to determine whether any of their public housing units must be removed from the public housing inventory per the required conversion policy.[80] This same assessment may be used by PHAs to determine whether or not to pursue voluntary conversion, although additional factors (the impact on residents, the surrounding community, and affordable housing) must be taken into account.

As of 2008, over 180,000 units of public housing had been removed through demolition or disposition and over 16,000 units had been removed through conversion.[81] (For more information on inventory removals, see Figure 2 later in this report.)

Eligibility, Rent, Terms of Occupancy

As noted earlier, the low-rent public housing program is governed by federal statute, regulation, and guidance, as well as local discretion and policy making. The following section of this report describes the federal rules and regulations that govern the basic aspects of the public housing program. However, given the amount of local discretion in the program, for any particular community the best place to learn a PHA's specific policies is the PHA's plans.

Eligibility

Today's public housing program is meant to provide assistance to low-income families,[82] so families must meet certain income standards in order to be eligible to live in public housing. In general, families must be low-income—having gross income at or below 80% of Area Median Income (AMI)[83]—at the time they apply to live in public housing. "Income" is defined in federal statute as income from all sources from all members of the household, including imputed income from assets, with some exceptions.[84]

Further, in order to be eligible the family must be comprised of citizens and/or eligible noncitizens.[85] If a family has "mixed status" (including members who are not citizens and not eligible non-citizens), then the family may live in public housing but the ineligible member is not permitted to receive assistance. This is accomplished by providing the family with a prorated benefit, which means the family must pay higher rent.[86]

Application, Waiting List, and Preferences

Families who wish to live in public housing must apply to their local PHA. Depending on the policies of the PHA, the household can apply to live in a specific property or any property within the PHA's inventory.[87] Some PHAs have designated properties as being available only to persons who are elderly or have a disability. Families who wish to live in such properties must be either elderly or have a disability.[88]

The demand for public housing is greater than the supply in most communities; as a result, a family is typically assigned to a waiting list once it applies for public housing. Waiting lists can be several months long, several years long, or even closed to new applicants. PHAs must establish policies related to how they will administer their waiting lists and include those policies in their annual plan. As a part of their waitlist management, PHAs may set local preferences, as long as those preferences are not in violation of federal civil rights law. Examples of allowable preferences include preferences for working families, families who are elderly or disabled, or veterans. Once a PHA has established preferences, it can then choose whether to apply, among families of the same preference category, a first-come, first-served selection policy or a random selection process.[89]

Targeting and Deconcentration

PHAs are charged with balancing two competing priorities in their public housing programs: serving the neediest families and deconcentrating poverty. Federal law requires that PHAs ensure that at least 40% of families admitted to public housing in a year are extremely low-income (defined as income at or below 30% of area median income).[90] At the same time, federal law also prohibits PHAs from concentrating very low-income families in public housing dwelling units in certain projects or buildings within projects.[91] PHAs are required to submit to HUD plans that explain how their admissions policies promote deconcentration of poverty and income mixing by bringing higher-income tenants into lower-income properties and lower-income tenants into higher-income properties.[92]

Screening

In addition to ensuring that families meet income eligibility standards, PHAs are also required to screen families to ensure that they are "suitable for tenancy."[93] Federal law prohibits PHAs from admitting household members who (1) have been convicted of producing methamphetamines on federally assisted housing property or (2) are subject to lifetime registration on a state sex offender registry.[94] Federal law also requires PHAs to prohibit admission for household members who (1) were evicted from federally assisted housing for participating in drug-related criminal activity in the prior three years and have not undergone rehabilitation, (2) are actively engaging in illegal drug use, or (3) have exhibited a pattern of illegal drug use.[95] These last three categories are subject to PHA interpretation, in that they leave discretion to the PHA to determine whether a family member has completed rehabilitation, is currently engaging in illegal drug use, or has exhibited a pattern of illegal drug use.

In addition to the federal prohibitions, PHAs may adopt additional discretionary screening criteria.[96] PHAs may establish policies that prohibit admission of households who have other criminal convictions, have poor credit histories, have poor rental histories, or who fail to meet other criteria set by the PHA. PHAs that choose to adopt elective screening criteria must ensure that the criteria are not discriminatory or in violation of the Fair Housing Act.

Rent

Federal housing law has generally defined housing as "affordable" to lower-income families if it costs no more than 30% of family income.[97] To ensure that the low-income families in public housing are paying affordable rents, federal law bases tenant rent on family income. In the public housing program, a family's rent is calculated as the highest of the following:

- 30% of the family's monthly *adjusted* income;
  - "Adjusted income" is total family income, less any deductions. Examples of deductions include
    - $480 for each dependent;
    - $480 for elderly or disabled households;
    - any unreimbursed medical expenses that exceed 3% of household income for elderly and disabled households;
    - certain child care expenses for working families with children;
    - in some cases, 100% of new earnings in the first year of new work and 50% of new earnings in the second year of new work, referred to as the earned income disregard;[98] and
    - additional deductions, at the discretion of the PHA.[99]
- 10% of the family's *gross* monthly income;
- welfare rent,[100] if applicable; or
- a minimum rent (up to $50) set by the PHA.[101]

Flat Rents

Each year, PHAs must provide each family living in public housing the option to pay a flat rent in lieu of an income-based rent. Flat rents are market comparable rents established by each PHA. The idea behind flat rents is to encourage families to increase their earnings; if a family's income increases, the family's rent does not increase under a flat-rent model. Any time that a family faces a decrease in income and paying flat rents becomes a financial hardship, the family may request to switch back to income-based rents.[102]

Utilities

Federal housing policy considers utilities to be a part of the housing costs of a family. Therefore, their costs are generally included when subsidizing tenants' housing costs. If a public housing development has individually metered units and the utilities are not included in the rent, then the PHA has the option to either pay a utility reimbursement directly to the family or pay the utility provider on behalf of the family. Each PHA is required to develop a schedule of utility allowances.[103] Those utility allowance schedules—which can be based on past patterns of consumption or other estimates of reasonable utility costs—are used to determine how much a PHA will pay toward a household's utility bills and to determine if households living in properties with PHA-paid utilities should pay an additional charge if they have excess consumption.[104]

Reexamination

Families' household composition and income are reexamined annually for rent determination purposes. Families are required to provide any necessary information and PHAs are required to obtain third party verification of family income, asset values, expenses related to deductions, and other factors. Families may request interim reexaminations if they have a change in income or family composition. PHAs must adopt policies governing interim reexaminations—such as whether families are required to report an increase in income or change in family size between annual reexaminations—and include those policies in their admissions and continued occupancy plans as well as in the lease.[105]

Community Service Requirement

At reexamination, families' compliance with the public housing community service and self-sufficiency requirement is also assessed. Under the requirement, non-elderly, non-disabled residents of public housing who are not otherwise exempted are required to participate in eight hours per month of either community service or economic self-sufficiency activities in order to retain their public housing.[106]

Termination of Tenancy

There are no federal time limits governing how long a family can live in public housing. As long as a family wishes to remain in public housing, and as long as they continue to pay their rent and comply with program rules, they can continue the residency.[107] PHAs are authorized to evict families whose incomes increase above the low-income limit, but they are not required to evict these "over-income" families.[108]

As is the case with screening, there are some federally determined, mandatory grounds for terminating tenancy or evicting families[109] and PHAs are also permitted to determine their own grounds for eviction. Federal law requires that PHAs terminate the assisted tenancy of any member of the household who is convicted of producing methamphetamine on federally assisted housing property.[110] PHAs are encouraged by HUD, but not required by law, to evict persons subject to lifetime registration on a state sex offender registry.[111]

Federal law also requires that PHAs adopt policies establishing that drug-related criminal activity, illegal drug use, or other criminal activity that threatens the health, safety, or right to peaceful enjoyment of other residents is grounds for termination of tenancy or assistance. In addition, PHAs are required to establish standards that allow termination of tenancy for alcohol abuse or provision of false information related to drug or alcohol abuse. PHAs may also establish additional grounds for termination of tenancy, such as other criminal conduct.

One important aspect of PHA discretion in termination cases relates to how it is applied. First, in most cases PHAs can determine when a household has met the threshold for termination of tenancy. Second, PHAs are permitted to determine whether the tenancy of the entire household should be terminated because of the actions of one member of the household, or even a guest of the household. PHAs have the discretion to request that an offending member be removed from the household, that an offending guest be barred from the property, or that the entire household's tenancy be terminated.[112]

Tenant Grievance Procedure

Tenants living in public housing are permitted to challenge decisions made by the PHA regarding tenants' individual circumstances as well as PHA policies that may adversely affect the tenants' rights, duties, welfare, or status. Each PHA is required to develop a written grievance procedure that includes both an informal process for resolving grievances as well as an informal hearing process.[113]

Additional Programs and Services

Resident Supports

The families served by the public housing program are low-income and some may have personal difficulties or other barriers that mean they could benefit from supportive services. While there is no dedicated source of funding for providing services for public housing residents, there are several programs through which PHAs can receive funding to hire staff to connect residents with services. The Resident Opportunity for Self Sufficiency (ROSS) program provides funding that PHAs can apply for to hire service coordinators to promote economic self-sufficiency among families and/or independent living for persons who are elderly or are living with disabilities. PHAs that wish to receive ROSS service coordinator funding apply to the Notice of Funding

Availability (NOFA) published by HUD each year in the *Federal Register*. The Public Housing Family Self Sufficiency (FSS) program is similar to the ROSS program in that it funds the hiring of service coordinators and uses the NOFA process.[114] The main difference is that the FSS program is specifically designed to link participating families to supportive services aimed at improving self-sufficiency. Families who agree to participate establish goals to be met within a five-year period and may be eligible to have any increased rent attributable to increased income deposited in an escrow account that they can access after five years. Some PHAs have service coordinator funding built into their operating funding.[115]

Section 3

Section 3 of the Housing and Urban Development Act of 1968, as amended, establishes a requirement that certain recipients of HUD funding, to the greatest extent feasible, provide job training, employment, and contracting opportunities for low- and very low-income individuals, including residents of public housing, in connection with HUD-funded projects and activities in their communities. The requirement specifically applies to all public housing funding, as well as other housing and community development funds spent on housing construction or rehabilitation. Under Section 3, PHAs and their contractors and subcontractors are required to make their best efforts, consistent with federal, state, and local laws and regulations, to give to low- and very low-income persons employment and training opportunities generated by funds from development assistance, operating assistance, and modernization assistance. These three categories encompass virtually all federal public housing funding received by PHAs. The act establishes priority categories for low- and very low-income families to whom such opportunities should be provided, with the first being residents of those developments for which the assistance is expended, the second being residents of other developments managed by the PHA, the third being participants in the Youthbuild program, and the fourth being low- and very low-income persons residing within the metropolitan area or non-metropolitan county.[116]

Public Housing Homeownership

PHAs are permitted to promote public housing resident homeownership in three ways: (1) by selling portions of public housing properties to residents, (2) by using some of their public housing capital funds to provide assistance to public housing residents wishing to become homeowners, or (3) by using some of their public housing capital funds to purchase homes to resell to public housing residents. PHAs that wish to pursue public housing homeownership must establish a plan that is then submitted to HUD for approval.[117] This option has not been widely used; as of May 2009, about 6,000 units of public housing had been sold to residents.

Moving to Work

The Moving to Work Demonstration (MTW) was authorized by Section 204 of the Omnibus Consolidated Rescissions and Appropriations Act of 1996 (P.L. 104-134).[118] The purpose of MTW was to provide HUD and PHAs the flexibility to design and test policies to

- reduce cost and achieve greater cost effectiveness in federal expenditures;
- give incentives to families with children where the head of household is working, seeking work, or is preparing for work by participating in job training, educational programs, or programs that assist people in obtaining employment and becoming economically self-sufficient; and
- increase housing choices for low-income families.

Under Moving To Work, up to 30 agencies could apply to HUD for waivers of most rules under the U.S. Housing Act of 1937 (P.L. 75-412).[119] With HUD approval, MTW agencies can merge their Section 8 voucher, public housing capital, and public housing operating funds; alter eligibility and rent policies, modify their funding agreements and reporting requirements with HUD, and make other changes.

Rules outside of the 1937 act, as amended—such as labor requirements and fair housing rules— cannot be waived under MTW, nor can rules governing the demolition and disposition of public housing. Agencies must also agree to serve substantially the same number of people they were serving before the demonstration and they must agree to continue to serve low-income families.

Agencies participating in MTW have used the flexibility it provides differently. Some have made minor changes to their existing Section 8 voucher and public housing programs, such as limiting reporting requirements; others have implemented full funding fungibility and significantly altered their eligibility and rent policies.[120]

TRENDS IN UNITS AND CHARACTERISTICS OF PROPERTIES

Determining the exact number of public housing units is complicated. The number of units under contract between HUD and a PHA at any given point in time is not necessarily the same as the number of physical units currently occupied by eligible families or available for occupancy. PHAs may be receiving funding for units that are temporarily vacant awaiting occupancy of a new tenant, temporarily vacant due to litigation, temporarily vacant awaiting rehabilitation, or permanently vacant awaiting demolition or disposition. There may also be units that are currently occupied that are slated for demolition or disposition and units that are in the process of being rehabilitated or built to replace units that were demolished or disposed of (sold or otherwise removed from the public housing inventory).

Generally, estimates of the current number of public housing units range from over 1.1 million units[121] to just under 1.2 million units.[122]

Figure 1 displays the trend over time in the number of public housing units eligible to receive payment. The public housing program peaked at just over 1.4 million units in the mid-1990s,[123] and the number of units has declined fairly steadily since. The public housing program today has about as many units as it did in the mid-1970s.

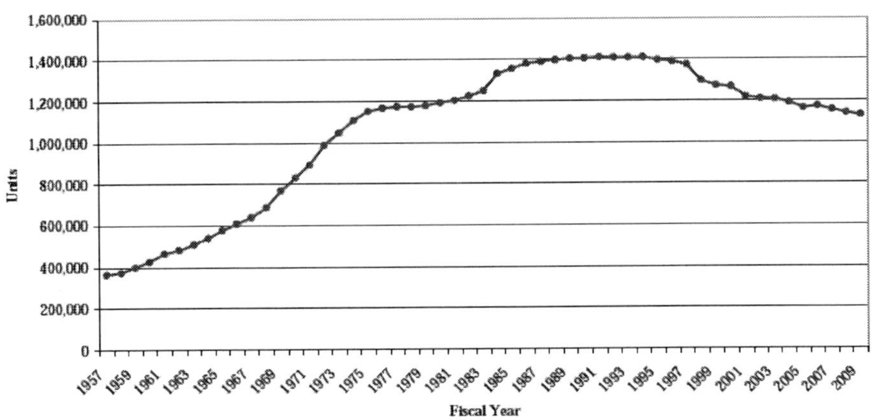

Source: HUD Congressional Budget Justifications, Units Eligible for Payment.

Figure 1. Public Housing Units Over Time 1957-2009.

The stock has been declining for two reasons: (1) PHAs have been demolishing and disposing of public housing units without fully replacing them; and (2) Congress has not authorized the addition of new units of public housing except to replace those being demolished and disposed of since the late 1990s.[124]

Between 1973 and May 2009, nearly 250,000 units of public housing were approved for removal from the public housing inventory and more than 200,000 were actually removed. As shown in Figure 2, the rate of removal has increased markedly since the mid-1990s, and the most common way a unit has been removed has been through demolition or disposition, although some units have been converted to vouchers. The rates of demolition and disposition increased markedly in the mid-1990s, which coincided with the creation of the HOPE VI program and the removal of the long-standing requirement that each unit of public housing that is removed from the inventory must be replaced (referred to as one-for-one replacement). According to HUD:

> Although demolition/disposition activity has always been permitted, HUD and its business partners have begun to actively pursue it as a management strategy option in the last ten years. This is due to the realization that some developments have difficulties associated not only with physical deterioration, but also with the overall deterioration of the surrounding community. It is also true that a large portion of the housing now being proposed for demolition/disposition was built in the late 1940s and early 1950s, and was built to a standard that is no longer acceptable for the general public. Developments meeting that description have very often become the housing of last resort within their communities.[125]

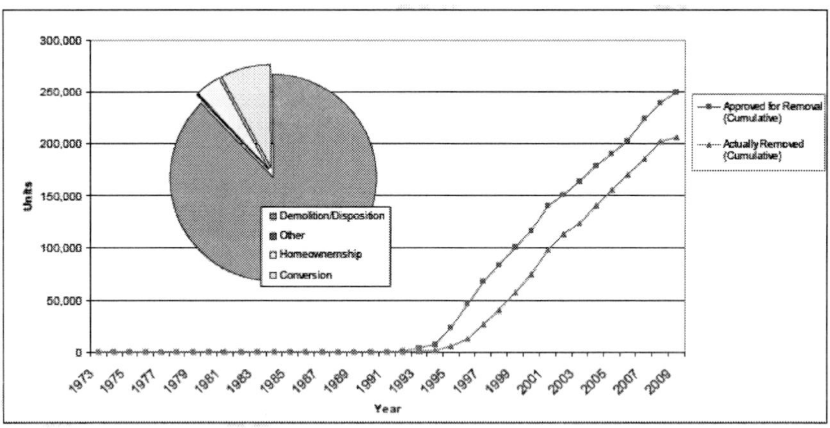

Source: CRS analysis of data provided by HUD.

Figure 2. Public Housing Units Removed from Inventory and Type of Removal 1973-May 2009.

Table 2. Public Housing Property Characteristics, 2009

Size and Age (Projects)	
Average Size	162 units
Median Size	111 units
Average Age	27 years
Average Bedroom Size	1.89 bedrooms
Building Type (Projects)	
Detached/semi-detached	17%
High-rise/mixed	23%
Row/townhouse	26%
Scattered site	22%
Walk-up/garden	13%
Occupancy Type (Projects)	
Family	64%
Elderly/disabled	36%
Location (Projects)	
Central city	41%
Non-central city	23%
Rural	36%
Census tract poverty concentrations	
0-20% poverty	49%
21-30% poverty	21%
31-40% poverty	13%
>40% poverty	18%

Source: HUD, Office of Public and Indian Housing, Real Estate Assessment Center, Financial Management Division, *Operating Fund Annual Report CY2009*, February 24, 2010.

The data presented in Table 2 provides descriptive information about public housing properties. Despite public housing's reputation as "the projects," epitomized by the largest developments in major cities, the most common form for today's public housing projects is notably smaller in scale; high-rise and mixed developments account for less than one-quarter of all public housing properties, while three-quarters of developments are row houses; townhomes; walk-up, garden style, detached, or semi-detached homes; and scattered site housing. Further, less than half of all public housing properties are in central city locations and nearly half are located in low-poverty census tracts.

It is important to note, however, that these data are at the property rather than the unit level.[126] Given that high-rise developments have greater density than other forms of housing and are more often located in central-city and high-poverty areas, the distribution of units is likely to be higher in these areas than that shown by the property data.

Figure 3 displays the geographic distribution of public housing across the country. States are shaded relative to the number of public housing units within their borders. Superimposed dots indicate the location of individual properties, with the relative size of the property reflected in the diameter of the dot. As shown in the map, New York has the greatest number of public housing units. New York is home to over 13% of the nation's public housing stock and has more than three times the number of units as the state with the next highest number of units (Pennsylvania, which has about 5.5% of the nation's public housing units). New York is also home to the largest public housing projects, with several having well over 2,000 units. While New York has the greatest number of units and the largest projects, both Texas and Pennsylvania have more public housing projects than New York. Overall, public housing is predominately located in the eastern half of the United States.

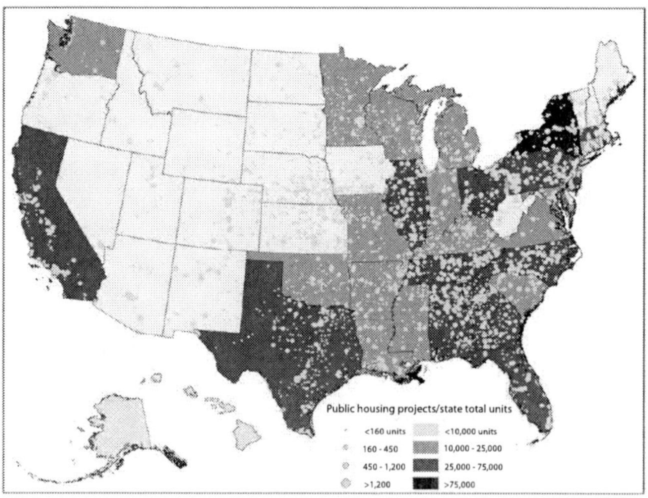

Source: Map prepared by CRS using data from HUD's Picture of Subsidized Housing 2008 dataset.

Figure 3. Geographic Location of Public Housing Properties and Units, 2008.

CHARACTERISTICS OF TENANTS

Unlike other social assistance programs that target specific subpopulations of low-income individuals and families (such as persons who are elderly, persons who are living with disabilities, or families with children), public housing is available to all types of low-income families and individuals. As shown in Figure 4, today's public housing program serves families headed by persons who are elderly, persons who have a disability, and persons who are not elderly and not living with a disability, with and without children. While no one household type accounts for the majority of public housing families, the most common household type in public housing is families headed by persons who are not elderly, not living with a disability, and have children. These families account for just over one-third of all households in public housing. Looking at the breakout of these families, the vast majority are comprised of single parent, female-headed households.

Elderly households without children are the second largest category, accounting for just under one-third of all households. Households where the head of household is living with a disability (including those both with and without children) account for about one-fifth of total households. Overall, there are more families without children (59% of all households) than with children (40%) in public housing.

The over 1.1 million families living in public housing are comprised of over 2 million people. The overall average household size in 2008 was 2.2 people; families with children tended to be larger (an average of 3.5 people per family) and families without children tended to be smaller (an average of 1.3 people per family). Of the over 2 million people living in public housing in 2008, about 40% were children under the age of 18 and about 16% were adults over the age of 62.

In terms of race and ethnicity, just under half of all households living in public housing in 2008 were headed by a person who identified his or her race as white, and just under half of all households were headed by a person who identified his or her race as black. Twenty-two percent of households were headed by a person who identified his or her ethnicity as Hispanic.

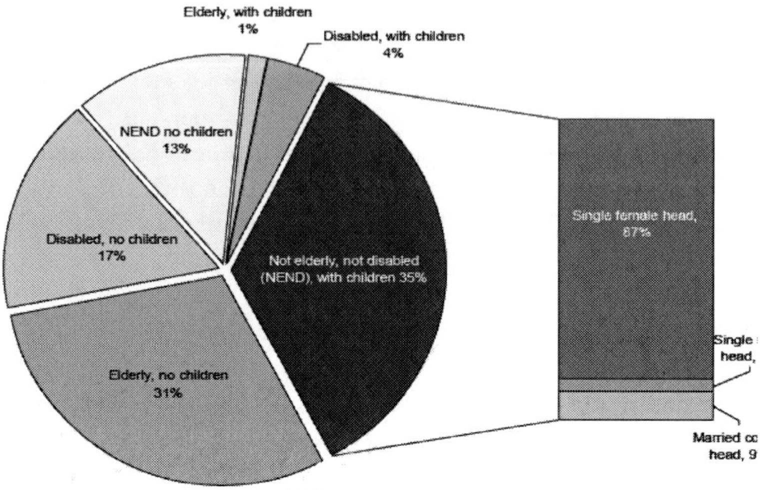

Source: CRS analysis of data provided by HUD.

Notes: Household types are derived by the elderly or disabled status of the household head. Totals may not add due to rounding.

Figure 4. Families in Public Housing by Household Type, 2008.

Table 3. Race and Ethnicity of Heads of Household, 2008

Head of Household Race	
White	49%
Black	48%
American Indian/Alaskan Native	1%
Asian Pacific Islander	2%
Head of Household Ethnicity	
Hispanic	22%
Non-Hispanic	78%

Source: CRS analysis of data provided by HUD.

With income restrictions on eligibility for public housing, households living in public housing are low-income. As shown in Table 4, the median family income of households living in public housing in 2008 was just over $9,000 per year. To give this number context, it can be compared to the national poverty guidelines, which are used to define who is "poor" and therefore may be eligible for a number of other social assistance programs.[127] Comparing the median income of all households to the two-person poverty guidelines for 2008 ($14,000),[128] the median income of families living in public housing was only about two-thirds of the poverty guideline. Comparing the median income of non-elderly, non-disabled families with children to the three-person poverty guidelines ($17,600),[129] median family income for these households was just over half of the poverty guideline in 2008.

Table 4. Median Income by Household Type, 2008

Head of Household Type	Median Gross Income
All households	$9,336
Elderly	$10,320
Disabled	$8,688
Not-Elderly, Not-Disabled (NEND) families w/o children	$8,892
NEND families with children	$9,000

Source: CRS analysis of HUD data

Note: Elderly and Disabled Household Types refer to the elderly status or non-elderly disabled status of the head of household. Those households may or may not have children.

Different types of families living in public housing receive their income from different sources. As shown in Table 5, in 2008 over 80% of all elderly households reported receiving income from Social Security or pensions. Most households headed by persons with disabilities reported receiving Supplemental Security Income (SSI) and/or other Social Security or pension income. Non-elderly, non-disabled families with children reported receiving income from a variety of sources. Over half reported income from work, nearly 40% reported some income from welfare (defined as payments from the Temporary Assistance for Needy Families (TANF) program or state General Assistance (GA) programs), and over one-fifth reported some income from child support payments. About 5% of all households reported receiving no income from any source.

Table 5. Source of Income by Household Type, 2008 (Percentages of households reporting any income from selected sources)

Household Type	Work	TANF or GA (Welfare)	Child Support	Supplemental Security Income	Social Security or Pension
Elderly	10	14	0	38	81
Disabled	12	26	3	63	51
NEND families w/o children	62	19	2	5	6
NEND families with children	56	39	21	9	6

Source: CRS analysis of HUD data

Note: Elderly and Disabled Household Types refer to the elderly status or non-elderly disabled status of the head of household. Those households may or may not have children.

Over the past several decades, social assistance programs have increasingly focused on promoting work and work activities among recipients of benefits, particularly non-elderly and non-disabled families. The community service and economic self-sufficiency requirement in public housing is an example of such a policy. Given the policy interest in increasing work effort among non-elderly, non-disabled families, Table 6 is provided to offer a closer look at the sources of income for these families. Looking at all non-elderly, non-disabled families, most families (more than two-thirds) received income from work. The majority of working families were not receiving welfare income (defined as TANF or GA) in 2008. Dividing this population into those with and without children, in both cases the plurality of families received income from work and not welfare, although families without children were receiving income from work at a higher rate than families with children. Twenty-two percent of not-elderly, not-disabled households received income from welfare but not from work, with those families with children more likely to receive income from welfare and not work. Given the work requirements in the federal TANF program, it is likely that most of those families receiving income from welfare are or will be subject to work requirements as a condition of receiving assistance. Just under one-fifth of NEND families with children, and nearly a quarter of NEND families without children, report receiving no income or receiving income only from non-work and non-welfare sources.

These families are the most likely to be subject to the community service requirement in public housing, assuming they are not otherwise exempt.

Table 6. Income from Welfare and Work Among Not-Elderly, Not-Disabled Families (NEND), 2008

Household Types	Work, No Welfare	Work and Welfare	Welfare, No Work	No Work, No Welfare
All NEND households	47%	11%	22%	20%
NEND with children	43%	13%	25%	19%
NEND without children	57%	5%	14%	24%

Source: CRS analysis of data from HUD.

As noted earlier in this report, families living in public housing pay income-based rents. Because the incomes of families living in public housing are quite low, the rents paid by those families are also quite low. As shown in Table 7, looking at all households, the median rent paid by tenants in 2008 was just over $200 per month. Non-elderly, non-disabled families with children paid the er $200), which is not surprising given that they tend to have the lowest incomes.

Table 7. Comparison of Rent Paid to Local Market Rents by Household Type, 2008

Household Type	Median Monthly Rent Paid by Household	Median Monthly Difference Between Rent Paid by Household and Local FMR
All households	210	510
Elderly	230	440
Disabled	210	450
NEND w/o children	220	460
NEND with children	190	640

Source: CRS analysis of HUD data

Note: Elderly and Disabled Household Types refer to the elderly status or non-elderly disabled status of the head of household. Those households may or may not have children.

In order to provide a sense of the financial benefits to families of living in public housing, Table 7 also compares the difference between what tenants pay in rent each month and the fair market rent (FMR) in their local communities.[130] In 2008, the median difference was $500 per month for all households. Not-elderly, not-disabled families with children had the greatest difference between the rents they pay to live in public housing and the local FMR, a benefit of over $640 per month or over $7,600 per year.

The public housing program does not impose limits on the length of time a family can live in public housing. Once a family is leasing a public housing unit, the family can continue to renew that lease until it is no longer eligible, either because the family's income increases too much to maintain eligibility or because the family violates program rules in some way. The data presented in Figure 5 provide a snapshot of the length of tenure of families living in public housing in September 2008. The bars provide a distribution of households by the number of years they have lived in public housing and household type, and the box in the center of the graph presents median and mean length of stay by household type. [131] More than half of all families living in public housing in 2008 had lived there for five years or less. The greatest share of households living in public housing had been in public housing for less than one year; the next greatest share had been living in public housing for 20 or more years. While families with children make up the greatest share of those families that have been living in public housing for less than one year, elderly-headed families make up the greatest share of those families that have been living in public housing for 20 or more years. Presumably, many of these elderly-headed families entered the program as a different household type, perhaps families with children, and their category changed as they aged.

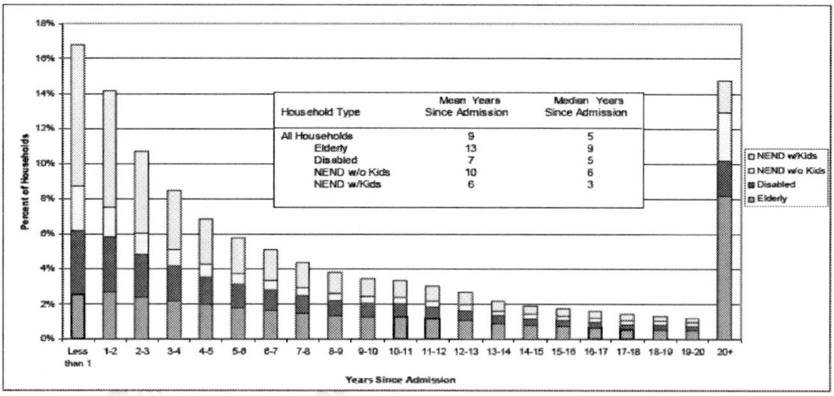

Source: CRS analysis of HUD data.

Notes: These data present point-in-time tenure data. Such point-in-time data cannot be used for a survival analysis (how long would a given person entering public housing be likely to stay).

Figure 5. Tenure by Household Type, 2008.

FUNDING

PHAs sustain public housing through a combination of federal funding, tenant rents, and other investment income. Congress typically appropriates several streams of funding to PHAs to help make up the difference between what PHAs receive in rent from tenants and what it costs to operate and maintain public housing. Operating funds are meant to fund the day-to-day operations of public housing (administration and staffing, utilities, routine maintenance, etc.). Capital funds are meant to help pay for modernization needs, such as replacing a roof or a heating and cooling system, or remodeling units. Both operating funds and capital funds are allocated to PHAs based on a formula. PHAs can also apply for competitive HOPE VI revitalization grants. HOPE VI grants are used to demolish and rebuild, or substantially rehabilitate, severely distressed public housing.

Operating Funding

Operating funds are meant to help pay for day-to-day operations, including utilities, safety and security measures, resident services, and administration. The operating fund provides subsidies to PHAs to make up the difference between what it costs to run public housing and what low-income tenants pay in rent. Under the formula, the calculation for determining a PHA's operating subsidy eligibility uses two components: expenses (meant to represent the cost of running public housing) and income (meant to represent the amount collected in tenant rents). HUD subtracts a PHA's income from its expenses, and the amount by which the income is short of the expenses is the PHA's operating subsidy eligibility.

For a number of years, the amount of appropriations provided by Congress was not sufficient to fund 100% of PHAs' formula eligibility; therefore, amounts provided to PHAs had to be prorated to fit within the amount of appropriations available. From 2005 to 2009, proration levels ranged from about 83% to about 89%.[132] In 2010, the operating fund proration level was over 100%.[133]

As previously noted, operating funds are meant to supplement the funds that PHAs receive from tenant rents, their own investments, and other sources. As a result, the percentage of a PHA's public housing operating budget that is made up of federal funds will vary across PHAs and from year to year. According to data from HUD, an estimated 57% of PHAs' expenditures nationally comes from federal operating funds, 38% comes from tenant rents, 2% comes from investment income, and 3% comes from other sources of income. HUD also provides estimates of how PHAs use their funds: 25% of PHA operating expenditures nationally covers the cost of utilities, 29% goes toward administrative expenses, 32% goes toward maintenance costs, 9% goes toward general expenses, and 2% each goes toward tenant services and protective services.[134]

Public Housing Drug Elimination Grants

The Public Housing Drug Elimination Grant program (PHDEP) was funded between FY1991- FY2001. The program initially provided competitive grant funding to PHAs, and later provided formula grants to PHAs, to be used for a variety of safety and security activities. Examples include funding for security guards or patrols, developing after-school program activities and other activities designed to reduce the use of drugs, and making physical changes to public housing to promote security (such as installing security cameras). When the program was ended, it was argued that all of the activities funded under PHDEP could also be funded using operating funding.[135]

Capital Funding

Capital funds are provided via formula to PHAs to help meet the modernization needs of public housing that cannot be met through the income collected via tenant rents. The formula for allocating capital funds uses various measures of relative need (e.g., size and age of stock) and relative construction costs. A portion of capital fund dollars is also generally set aside to provide Replacement Housing Factor (RHF) funding, which is funding set aside to replace units that are demolished or disposed of.[136]

PHAs may use their capital fund dollars for the modernization and development of public housing and for management improvements.[137] Additionally, up to 20% of capital funds may be transferred to supplement their operating funding.[138]

The most recent study (which is more than a decade old now[139]) of the modernization needs of public housing found that PHAs accumulated roughly $2 billion in capital needs each year, and that there was a backlog of $18 billion-$20 billion in unmet needs.[140] Since that study was done, many public housing units have been demolished or redeveloped; at the same time, appropriation levels have only hovered around the annual accrual needs level[141] (see Table 8 for recent funding levels). As a result, it is unclear what the current capital needs are in public housing. In the FY2008 appropriations act,[142] Congress directed HUD to conduct a new Capital Needs Assessment in order to obtain a more current estimate of the capital needs of public housing.

Leveraging and Mixed Finance Development

An increasing number of PHAs are leveraging their capital funds to secure outside resources to address their capital needs. According to data available from HUD, as of June 2010 over $3 billion had been approved to be leveraged by over 200 PHAs.[143] Under these transactions, PHAs pledge a portion of their future year annual capital funds toward the debt service payments on a loan or a bond. The pledge of future capital funds is made subject to the availability of appropriations, and the loans and bonds secured by the pledge are not backed by the federal government. PHAs wishing to participate in the Capital Fund Financing program (CFFP), the pilot program through which HUD has permitted these transactions, must apply for prior HUD approval. HUD generally restricts PHAs to pledging no more than one-third of their capital funding toward meeting the debt service needs of a bond or loan. PHAs are not currently permitted to pledge their operating funding or mortgage their public housing properties.[144]

HOPE VI

HOPE VI is a public housing redevelopment grant program. Through HOPE VI, HUD provides competitive grants to PHAs to rehabilitate or demolish public housing and replace it generally with mixed-income housing.

HOPE VI began as a demonstration program, created in reaction to the findings of the National Commission on Severely Distressed Public Housing. The commission's 1992 report labeled 6% of the public housing stock as severely distressed; at the time, this equaled 86,000 units. These severely distressed properties were characterized by high crime, low employment and few opportunities for residents, and poor physical conditions.

The purpose of the HOPE VI program is to revitalize severely distressed public housing developments and transform them into safe, livable environments. As described by HUD, this includes changing the physical characteristics of public housing from high-rise tenements to attractive, marketable units that blend in with the surrounding neighborhoods; lessening concentrations of poverty by reducing density and promoting mixed-income communities; encouraging partnerships with other agencies and local governments for support and resources; achieving high-quality management in public housing and enforcing strict eviction rules; and helping residents to attain self-sufficiency by providing services and educational opportunities, and by encouraging economic development in the area surrounding public housing.

The program was initially funded in FY1993 and has been funded each year since, although the overall funding level has declined in recent years (see Table 8 for recent funding levels). HOPE VI revitalization grants are awarded on a competitive basis to PHAs that apply for such grants. Through FY2009, HUD had awarded 260 revitalization grants.

While the program has been credited with demolishing some of the most troubled public housing and replacing it with higher quality, mixed-income housing, it has also been criticized for the ways in which it has displaced existing residents. The Obama Administration has proposed replacing the HOPE VI program with a new initiative, referred to as Choice Neighborhoods, which would expand the concept of HOPE VI beyond public housing to other distressed neighborhoods and increase requirements related to tenant relocation.

Recent Trends in Funding

As can be seen in Table 8, total funding for public housing has fluctuated up and down over the last decade. Total funding was increasing until FY2002. From FY2002 through FY2006, total public housing funding steadily declined, most rapidly following large reductions in funding for HOPE VI, which was slated for elimination by the George W. Bush Administration (and later, by the Obama Administration). Beginning with FY2007, funding began to rise again; apart from the $4 billion in stimulus capital funding provided in FY2009 by the American Recovery and Reinvestment Act (ARRA; P.L. 111-5), FY2010 total funding for public housing was at the highest level since the modern funding system for the program was adopted.

Looking at appropriations relative to the number of public housing units eligible for payment in Figure 6, it appears that per unit funding remained relatively flat[145] from FY1999 through FY2008, with some increases in early years (commensurate with increases in appropriations) and some decreases (commensurate with periods of appropriations decreases). The sharp rise in funding per unit in FY2009 is primarily attributable to the $4 billion in capital funding provided in the economic stimulus legislation.

Table 8. Appropriations for Public Housing, FY1999-FY2010 (dollars in millions)

FY	Operating Fund	Capital Fund	Drug Elimination Grants[a]	HOPE VI	Total Public Housing
1999	2,818	3,000	310	625	6,753
2000	3,138	2,900	310	575	6,923
2001	3,242	3,000	310	575	7,127
2002	3,495	2,843	0	574	6,912
2003	3,577	2,712	0	570	6,859
2004	3,579	2,696	0	149	6,424
2005	2,438[c]	2,579	0	143	5,160[c]
2006	3,564	2,439	0	99	6,102
2007	3,864	2,439	0	99	6,402
2008	4,200	2,439	0	100	6,739
2009	4,455	6,450[b]	0	120	11,025
2010	4,775	2,500	0	200	7,475

Source: HUD Congressional Budget Justifications, FY2001-FY2009. Enacted funding figures taken from subsequent years' justifications.

[a] Drug elimination grants were funded and awarded from FY1991-FY2001. They were initially available to PHAs competitively, and then via formula allocation later.

[b] Includes $4 billion in emergency funding provided by the American Recovery and Reinvestment Act of 2009 (P.L. 111-5).

[c] An accounting change enacted by Congress led to a one-time savings in the public housing operating fund in FY2005. For more information, see discussion on p. 13 of CRS Report RL32443, *The Department of Housing and Urban Development (HUD): FY2005 Budget*.

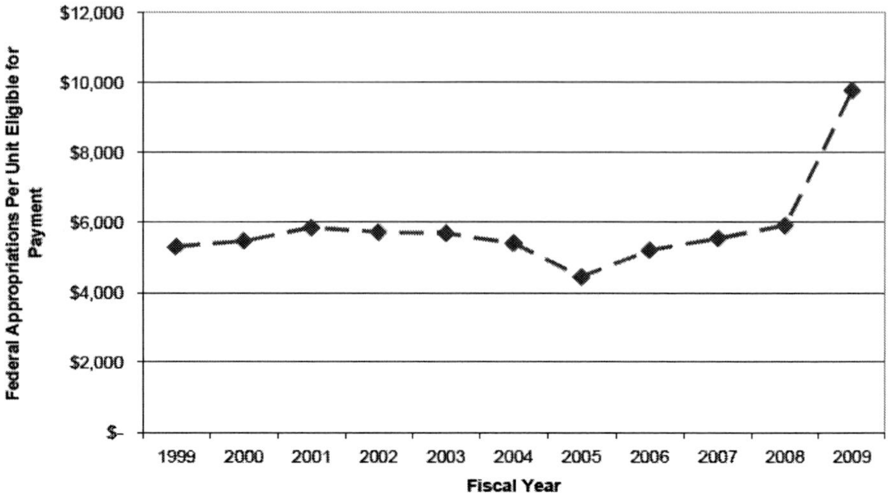

Source: See Table 8 and Figure 1.

Notes: As noted in Table 7, there was a drop in funding in FY2005 resulting from one-time budget savings that did not affect the overall program level. As a result, the decline in per unit funding in FY2005 does not accurately portray the amount of funding available in that fiscal year.

Figure 6. Funding per Unit, FY1999-FY2009 (nominal dollars).

POLICY ISSUES

While the purpose of this report is to provide an overview of and background information about the public housing program, it is important to also note that a number of policy issues about the program have been raised in recent years and have been and may be considered by Congress. While not fully addressed in this report, several of these issues are summarized below.

Funding Levels

There is an acknowledged backlog of unmet capital needs in the nation's public housing stock. The majority of the public housing stock is several decades old and much of the stock has not had the level of ongoing maintenance and major rehabilitation needed to keep it viable and habitable. Complicating matters, in some cases, is that properties were not built in such a way as to promote long-term viability (in some cases due to the use of poor quality materials or poor design, perhaps resulting from low per unit cost caps). The declining physical state of the public housing stock may be due in part to federal funding levels that, paired with federal rent collection rules, left PHAs with inadequate budgets to meet their properties' capital needs. In some cases, it may also be due to poor management decisions at the local level. Regardless of the cause, there is an acknowledged backlog of unmet capital needs in public housing that current federal funding levels, unless they increase substantially, are unlikely to address (notwithstanding the one-time increase in funding provided in the economic stimulus legislation in FY2009). As properties fall into disrepair, they are more likely to be candidates for removal from the public housing stock through demolition, disposition, or conversion.

The HOPE VI program was designed, in part, to address the unmet capital needs of those properties that are in the worst condition. As HOPE VI grants became smaller, leveraging expectations increased and PHAs began using their HOPE VI grant funding to secure additional private financing. Today, many PHAs have become adept at leveraging private resources, even without HOPE VI grants, by pledging other federal funding, primarily their capital funding. However, there are limits to the extent that PHAs can access these private mixed-finance markets. In order to prevent PHAs from becoming over-leveraged, HUD limits the share of future capital funding PHAs can pledge toward repaying debt. PHAs are further limited in that they are not currently permitted to pledge their future operating fund dollars to repay debt, nor are they permitted to pledge the underlying property itself as security to leverage private funding. Additionally, PHAs seeking funding in the private market are dependent on the willingness of lenders to provide them with capital on terms that are agreeable.

If there is a policy desire to preserve the existing public housing stock, additional funding would likely be needed. This could come in the form of increased federal appropriations. The economic stimulus legislation in the 111th Congress provided one of the largest infusions of capital funding for public housing in recent years. At nearly $4 billion dollars, it should have been sufficient to address around 20% of the estimated backlog in capital needs ($18 billion-$20 billion). These funds were designated as emergency supplemental funding, meant to stimulate the economy during the recession, and were therefore provided outside of the budget constraints of the regular annual appropriations process; it is unclear if similar future infusions will be forthcoming. In light of tight budget constraints and political questions about the popularity of the public housing program, future large infusions of federal funding are uncertain.

Federal rent policies could be changed to allow PHAs to collect higher payments from tenants. However, such a change would violate current standards of affordability and it is unclear, given the extremely low incomes of residents, if they could pay additional rent sufficient to meet unmet capital needs. Other options include making changes to existing policies to allow PHAs to better access private capital markets. These options could include permitting PHAs to leverage their operating fund dollars, permitting PHAs to mortgage the underlying value of their public housing properties, and/or creating instruments, such as mortgage insurance programs through the Federal Housing Administration (FHA), to encourage or provide incentives to lenders to make loans to PHAs on favorable terms.

The Obama Administration, as well as the 111th Congress, also introduced proposals designed to increase PHAs' abilities to access private capital. The Transforming Rental Assistance Initiative proposed in the President's FY2011 budget request would change the way that public housing is funded to permit PHAs to access private capital, in part by removing the limitations on mortgaging public housing properties. The proposal, renamed Preserving, Enhancing, and Transforming Rental Assistance (PETRA) in draft legislation circulated by the Administration, proved controversial with low-income housing advocates who were concerned that PETRA would lead to the "privatization" of public housing and therefore the loss of its long-term affordability.[146] In contrast, the Public Housing Reinvestment and Tenant Protection Act of 2010 (H.R. 5814, 111th Congress), which was ordered to be reported by the House Financial Services Committee, proposed to authorize HUD through the FHA to insure notes or other obligations issued by PHAs to finance the rehabilitation of public housing.

While neither PETRA nor H.R. 5814 was enacted before the close of the 111th Congress, both may be considered in the 112th Congress. A version of the Public Housing Reinvestment and Tenant Protection Act has been introduced (H.R. 762) and a version of the President's Transforming Rental Assistance proposal was included in the President's FY2012 budget request.

The Role of Public Housing

In light of the decline in the number of public housing units over time and the lack of authority to construct new units, the future role of the public housing program in federal housing policy is uncertain. The public housing program began as a construction program designed to help stimulate the economy coming out of the Great Depression. Its role evolved over time: first, to meet housing shortages during and after World War II; later, to address shortages of decent housing in conjunction with Urban Renewal efforts; and finally, to address shortages of decent housing that was affordable to the poorest families. In this last role, as a provider of affordable housing to poor families, the program has declined in prominence as other models of providing direct housing assistance to the poor have been developed. First, there were programs promoting the construction of properties owned by private market participants (through FHA insurance programs and later Section 8 rental assistance contracts), and later there were programs subsidizing families' housing costs in the existing housing stock (through the Section 8 voucher program). This last model, the Section 8 voucher program, is the only direct rental assistance program serving poor families that has grown to serve more families in the last several decades. At least part of that growth is attributable to declines in the number of public housing units, as families being displaced from public housing have received vouchers. These other models were developed in direct response to perceived shortcomings—lack of mobility, cost effectiveness, and efficiency—in the public housing program.

With policies like mandatory and voluntary conversion of public housing to vouchers, the question may be raised as to whether the "vouchering-out" of public housing is an inevitability, or if public housing itself is valuable enough to warrant taking steps to preserve it. Critics of public housing point to its often poor locations and conditions and argue that it traps the most vulnerable families in the worst housing conditions. They point to high rates of crime at some developments and low levels of social capital development and work effort, contending that public housing denies poor families choice and the option to live in communities of opportunity. Moreover, it is argued that the rent structure does little to promote self-sufficiency and may even discourage it. Advocates for public housing argue that the most vulnerable families are the least likely to have their needs met by the private market, even with a Section 8 rental voucher. Landlords are not required to accept vouchers and are permitted to screen families for suitability. PHAs, on the other hand, have a social mission to serve the poorest families. Further, advocates contend that high-quality public housing, particularly when it is enriched with services, can itself provide opportunities for families. They point to successful HOPE VI mixed-income communities and research on how place-based interventions can promote family success, particularly for persons who are elderly, but also for families with children.

In addition to the policy arguments for and against preserving public housing, the issue of cost is relevant. In recent years, the average annual "cost" to the federal government of providing a voucher to a family has been greater than the per unit funding provided to public housing.[147] This could serve to bolster arguments in favor of retaining public housing as a more cost-effective way of providing rental assistance to low-income families. However, the low cost of public housing reflects what most agree is an underfunding of public housing. If public housing was funded at its full funding needs—particularly in light of the backlog of capital needs—the cost to the federal government of public housing would likely be much higher, and potentially higher than the cost of vouchers. However, in order to fully evaluate the costs and benefits of public housing one may wish to consider the underlying value of the public housing properties themselves, which were built with federal assistance and maintained with federal funds. Questions about to whom that value belongs may also be considered when evaluating the costs and benefits of the program in light of potential changes. These questions about underlying value, which are beyond the scope of this report, may be difficult to answer and different observers may come to different conclusions.

End Notes

[1] While the low-rent public housing program was not authorized until the Housing Act of 1937, the federal government, through the Recovery Finance Corporation and Housing Division of the Public Works Administration, built roughly 21,800 units of low-rent housing between 1932-1937. The majority of these units were transferred to the public housing stock. Robert Moore Fisher, *Twenty Years of Public Housing* (New York, NY: Harper and Brothers Publishers, 1959), Chapter 4. (Cited hereafter as Fisher).

[2] For more information about the origins of public housing, see Elizabeth Wood, *The Beautiful Beginnings, The Failure to Learn: Fifty Years of Public Housing in America*, National Center for Housing Management, October 1982, Chapter 1; and Fisher, Chapter 1.

[3] Lawrence Vale, *From the Puritans to the Projects: Public Housing and Public Neighbors* (Cambridge, MA: Harvard University Press, 2000), Chapter 3.

[4] This war worker housing was eventually converted to public housing by the Housing Act of 1950.

[5] Ibid.

[6] Housing and Home Finance Agency, 16th Annual Report, 1962, p. 212.

[7] Fisher, Chapter 6.

[8] See Alexander von Hoffman, "A Study in Contradictions: The Origins and Legacy of the Housing Act of 1949," Fannie Mae Foundation, Housing Policy Debate, vol. 11, issue 12,

2000; and Elizabeth Wood, *The Beautiful Beginnings, The Failure to Learn: Fifty Years of Public Housing in America*, National Center for Housing Management, October 1982, Chapter 2.

[9] See Alexander von Hoffman, "A Study in Contradictions: The Origins and Legacy of the Housing Act of 1949," Fannie Mae Foundation, Housing Policy Debate, vol. 11, issue 12, 2000, p. 315.

[10] Fisher, Table 7.

[11] Elizabeth Wood, *The Beautiful Beginnings, The Failure to Learn: Fifty Years of Public Housing in America*, National Center for Housing Management, October 1982, p. 44.

[12] Fisher, Table 1, p. 14. This number includes only those units built under the authority of the 1949 act; it does not include all of the units created under the previous authorities.

[13] Elizabeth Wood, *The Beautiful Beginnings, The Failure to Learn: Fifty Years of Public Housing in America*, National Center for Housing Management, October 1982, p. 67.

[14] For more information about these programs, see CRS Report RL34591, *Overview of Federal Housing Assistance Programs and Policy*.

[15] Richard F. Muth, *Public Housing: An Economic Evaluation*, American Enterprise Institute for Public Policy Research, Washington, DC, 1973, pp. 44-45.

[16] Figures from the beginning of the decade taken from the 16th Annual Report of the Housing and Home Finance Agency, 1962; figures from the end of the decade taken from Richard F. Muth, *Public Housing: An Economic Evaluation*, American Enterprise Institute for Public Policy Research, Washington, DC, 1973, p. 13

[17] See Alexander von Hoffman, "A Study in Contradictions: The Origins and Legacy of the Housing Act of 1949," Fannie Mae Foundation, Housing Policy Debate, vol. 11, issue 12, 2000, p. 315.

[18] For an illustration of the troubled history of race in public housing, see Lawrence Vale, *From the Puritans to the Projects: Public Housing and Public Neighbors* (Cambridge, MA: Harvard University Press, 2000), Chapter 4.

[19] P.L. 90-448

[20] P.L. 91-152

[21] Richard F. Muth, *Public Housing: An Economic Evaluation*, American Enterprise Institute for Public Policy Research, Washington, DC, 1973, p. 18.

[22] From 1955 to 1972, the percentage of families not receiving public assistance declined from over 70% to just 25%. "The Report of the Task Force on Improving the Operation of Federally Insured or Financed Housing Programs, Volume II: Public Housing," National Center for Housing Management, 1973, p. 12.

[23] P.L. 91-609

[24] An exception was made for the Section 202 Housing for the Elderly program.

[25] For more information, see President Richard M. Nixon, State of the Union Message to Congress on Community Development, March 8, 1973.

[26] While public housing construction restarted as Congress authorized funding for new units, the moratorium effectively ended the contracting for and construction of new units under the Section 236 and Section 221(d)(3) programs.

[27] P.L. 93-383.

[28] A reservation reflects a commitment to build or put under contract a unit of public housing. Not all reserved units are necessarily built or occupied eventually.

[29] CRS Report 91-369E, *Trends in Funding and Numbers of Households in HUD-Assisted Housing, Fiscal Years 1975-1991*, by Grace Milgrim (out of print but available upon request to CRS).

[30] P.L. 97-35.

[31] Up to 5% of new units and 10% of existing units each year could be provided to families with income between 50% and 80% of area median income.

[32] Under federal preferences, applicants who met certain criteria (such as living in substandard housing) were to be given preference in admission and selection for assistance over other families. Congress suspended the system of federal preferences each year in annual appropriations acts beginning in 1996; federal preferences were repealed by P.L. 105-276.

[33] P.L. 98-181

[34] P.L. 100-242

[35] The 1983 act (P.L. 98-181) had repealed authority for new contracts under the prior forms of Section 8.

[36] P.L. 100-242

[37] CRS Report LTR 83-1647, *Trends in Funding and Numbers of Households in HUD-Assisted Housing, Fiscal Years 1974-1984*, by Grace Milgrim (out of print but available upon request to CRS).

[38] P.L. 101-235

[39] P.L. 101-625

[40] P.L. 100-550

[41] U.S. Department of Housing and Urban Development (HUD), "HUD Reinvention: From Blueprint to Action," March 1995.

[42] According to testimony of John C. Weicher, Assistant Secretary for Housing-Federal Housing Commissioner-Designate, U.S. Department of Housing and Urban Development (HUD), before the Senate Committee on Banking, Housing and Urban Affairs, May 15, 2001: "[T]here were numerous proposals from Republican members of Congress to abolish HUD, among them: a group of freshmen Congressmen; Sen. Faircloth, who was chairman of the HUD Oversight subcommittee of this Committee; and Sen. Dole, the majority leader and leading Presidential candidate. [] In 1996, the Republican platform included a plank to abolish HUD."

[43] The Personal Responsibility and Work Opportunity Reconciliation Act of 1996 (PRWORA; P.L. 104-193) abolished the Aid to Families with Dependent Children (AFDC) program, which had provided a cash assistance entitlement to low-income families. PRWORA replaced AFDC with the Temporary Assistance for Needy Families (TANF) program, a flexible block grant to states that required states to implement time limits and work requirements for cash assistance recipients. For more information, see CRS Report RS20807, *Short History of the 1996 Welfare Reform Law*, by Joe Richardson and Vee Burke.

[44] See 42 U.S.C. 1437g(g)(3)

[45] Christopher Logan, Hin-Kin Lam, and Seth Cooper, et al., *Analysis of Total Development Costs in Public Housing*, Abt Associates, Inc., for U.S. Department of Housing and Urban Development (HUD), Final Report, Washington, DC, July 1998, p. 1.

[46] Net new development refers to the development of additional units of housing, as opposed to units built to replace other units that were demolished or disposed of.

[47] American Recovery and Reinvestment Act of 2009, P.L. 111-5.

[48] U.S. Department of Housing and Urban Development (HUD), Public Housing Occupancy Guidebook, http://www.hud.gov/offices/pih/programs/ph/rhiip/phguidebook.cfm.

[49] 42 U.S.C. 1437(b).

[50] Some PHAs also own and manage state-funded, non-federal public housing. In the early years of the public housing program, some states—including Massachusetts and New York—

developed their own state-funded public housing. State-funded public housing is not under contract with the federal government, and therefore it does not receive federal funding and is not subject to federal program rules. Over the years, many units of state-funded public housing have been "federalized" by Congress and HUD, meaning they have been absorbed into the public housing stock.

[51] For more information on the Section 8 voucher program, see CRS Report RL32284, *An Overview of the Section 8 Housing Programs: Housing Choice Vouchers and Project-Based Rental Assistance*, by Maggie McCarty.

[52] Bruce Katz and Margery Austin Turner, "Who Should Run the Housing Voucher Program? A Reform Proposal," Working paper prepared for the Brookings Institution Center on Urban and Metropolitan Policy, November 2000. This report is focused on PHA consolidation for the purposes of the Section 8 voucher program.

[53] In his FY2008 budget request, President Bush requested up to $5 million for a PHA bonus fund to encourage PHA consolidation. HUD's Congressional Budget Justifications argued that consolidation of small PHAs would lead to greater efficiencies. The bonus fund was not enacted by Congress.

[54] The Obama Administration's Preserving, Enhancing and Transforming Rental Assistance (PETRA) proposal, discussed briefly later in this report, initially included priority in consideration for funding applications to PHAs that had voluntarily chosen to consolidate.

[55] 24 C.F.R. 903.13

[56] 24 C.F.R. 903.19

[57] Such as a community's Consolidated Plan, which is required to be developed as a condition of receiving HUD grant funds such as Community Development Block Grant (CDBG) funds.

[58] 24 C.F.R. 903.23

[59] HUD published implementing guidance on November 13, 2008, in PIH Notice 2008- 41(HA), "Public Housing Agency (PHA) Five-Year and Annual Plan Process for all PHAs."

[60] 24 C.F.R. 964.135

[61] 24 C.F.R. 964 et seq.

[62] 24 C.F.R. 964.150.

[63] PHAS is governed by regulations at 24 C.F.R. 902 et.seq.

[64] High performers may be eligible for bonus funding under the Public Housing Capital Fund. For more details, see 24 C.F.R. 905.10(j).

[65] 42 U.S.C 1437d(j)(3)(B)(I).

[66] 24 C.F.R. 902.75.

[67] Section 565 of the Quality Housing and Work Responsibility Act of 1998 (QHWRA; P.L. 105-276) revised and expanded HUD's powers for dealing with troubled PHAs (codified at 42 U.S.C. 1437d (j)(3)).

[68] 24 C.F.R. § 902.83

[69] The ACC is the contract between a PHA and HUD under which the PHA agrees to administer its public housing program in accordance with federal rules in exchange for receiving federal funding.

[70] HUD may determine that a PHA is in "substantial default" if it is acting in violation of federal statute, if it is in violation of its contract with HUD, or if it has been deemed troubled but has not shown substantial improvement. (24 C.F.R. § 902.79)

[71] In some cases, a court may find a PHA in violation of its Annual Contributions Contract, and may choose to place the PHA in a court-ordered and designed "judicial receivership."

[72] For more information, see CRS Congressional Distribution Memo, *Public Housing Authority (PHA) Receiverships*, by Maggie McCarty (contact the author for a copy), July 11, 2008;

and U.S. Government Accountability Office (GAO), *Information on Receiverships at Public Housing Authorities*, GAO 03-363.

[73] Based on data available from HUD at http://www.hud.gov/offices/pih/programs/hcv/ogddata/lowrent-s8-units.zip and accessed in October 2010.

[74] The use restrictions associated with the annual contributions contracts renew each year when a PHA accepts public housing funding through the capital and operating funds (described later in this report). Property acquired or developed with funds from the U.S. Housing Act of 1937 must be operated as public housing for a 40-year period that begins on the date on which the project becomes available for occupancy, as determined by HUD. This 40-year period is extended if PHA receives other funding, such as Capital Funds or Operating Funds.... Property modernized or receiving assistance of Capital Funds from the U.S. Housing Act of 1937 must be operated and maintained as public housing for a 20-year period that begins on the latest date on which modernization is complete or assistance is provided with Capital Funds covered by the Capital Fund ACC Amendment. The 20-year requirement may extend the use of the property as public housing beyond the original 40-year ACC requirement or beyond any requirement incurred as a result of receiving Operating Funds.... Property that receives Operating Funds from the U.S. Housing Act of 1937 must be operated as public housing for a 10-year period beginning upon the conclusion of the fiscal year for which such amounts were provided. The 10-year requirement may extend the use of the property as public housing beyond the original 40-year ACC requirement or beyond any requirement incurred as a result of receiving Capital Funds. U.S. Department of Housing and Urban Development (HUD), http://www.hud.gov/offices/pih/centers/sac/demo_dispo/

[75] 24 C.F.R. 970.15

[76] 24 C.F.R. 970.19.

[77] However, demolitions and dispositions under Section 18 of the U.S. Housing Act are not subject to the Uniform Relocation Act (24 C.F.R. 270.21(g); regulations governing the URA can be found at 49 C.F.R. Part 24).

[78] 24 C.F.R. 970.21.

[79] Section 202 of the Omnibus Consolidated Rescissions and Appropriations Act of 1996 (P.L. 104-134).

[80] HUD published final rules implementing QHWRA's required and voluntary conversion requirements in the *Federal Register* on September 17, 2003, with an effective date of March 15, 2004. However, the rules were inoperable, as a separate cost methodology for undertaking the assessment of properties for cost-effectiveness was not available. HUD published the final cost comparison methodology on March 20, 2006.

[81] Based on data provided to CRS by HUD.

[82] For the purposes of the public housing program, a "household" is defined as a family, including, where appropriate, a live-in aide (24 C.F.R. 5.100). A "family" is defined as including, but not limited to, a family with or without children, an elderly family, a near-elderly family, a disabled family, and the remaining member of a tenant family, and a single person who is not an elderly or displaced person, or a person with disabilities, or the remaining member of a tenant family (24 C.F.R. 5.403). This is the extent of the HUD guidance on the subject. Individual PHAs may add further clarification in their Admissions and Continued Occupancy plans, for example, defining a family as a group of individuals who have evidenced a stable family relationship. The terms family and household are used interchangeably in this report.

[83] HUD establishes income limits, based on area median incomes, for all metropolitan areas and counties in the country each year and publishes those limits on the department's website.

[84] There are some forms of income that are statutorily excluded from income for the purpose of housing programs. Examples include income earned by full-time students under age 18, foster care maintenance payments, and the value of food stamps. See 24 C.F.R. 5.609.

[85] 24 C.F.R. Part 5, Subpart E.

[86] For more information, see CRS Report RL31753, *Immigration: Noncitizen Eligibility for Needs-Based Housing Programs*, by Alison Siskin and Maggie McCarty.

[87] If a PHA wishes to implement site-based waiting lists rather than central waiting lists, it must include that policy in its annual plan and HUD will approve the change as a part of the annual plan review. PHAs with site-based waiting lists must ensure that their policies are in accordance with fair housing law and meet other requirements. See 24 C.F.R. 903.7(b)(2).

[88] If a PHA wants to change the composition of a building to only elderly residents, it must submit a plan to HUD to ask for approval. If the plan is approved, PHAs cannot evict non-elderly residents with disabilities, although PHAs may help residents relocate if they want to move. The law also requires that if a PHA is unable to rent an available unit to an elderly household within 60 days, it must make the unit available to near-elderly tenants (where the head of household or spouse is age 50 or older). If the unit cannot be rented to near-elderly families, then it must be made available to all families. For more information on housing for persons who are elderly, see CRS Report RL33508, *Section 202 and Other HUD Rental Housing Programs for Low-Income Elderly Residents*, by Libby Perl.

[89] 24 C.F.R. 960.206

[90] 42 U.S.C. 1437n(a)(2). PHAs that also administer a voucher program may be able to reduce this targeting requirement if they exceed the targeting requirement in the voucher program. See 24 C.F.R. 960.202(b).

[91] 42 U.S.C. 1437n(a)(3).

[92] See 24 C.F.R. Part 903, Subpart A for more information on the Deconcentration Plan.

[93] 24 C.F.R. 960.203(c).

[94] 42 U.S.C. 13663.

[95] 42 U.S.C. 13661-13662.

[96] 24 C.F.R. 960.203

[97] For a history of the evolution of the concept and definition of housing affordability, see Danilo Pelletiere, "Getting to the Heart of Housing's Fundamental Question: How Much Can a Family Afford? A Primer on Housing Affordability Standards in U.S. Housing Policy," National Low Income Housing Coalition, February 2008.

[98] For more information about the earned income disregard, see 24 C.F.R. 960.225.

[99] Historically, PHAs have not been reimbursed by HUD for the costs of discretionary deductions.

[100] 42 U.S.C. 1437a: "[if] the family is receiving payments for welfare assistance from a public agency and a part of such payments, adjusted in accordance with the family's actual housing costs, is specifically designated by such agency to meet the family's housing costs, the portion of such payments which is so designated."

[101] 24 C.F.R. 5.628

[102] 24 C.F.R. 960.253(b)

[103] The utilities for which allowances may be provided include electricity, natural gas, propane, fuel oil, wood or coal, and water and sewage service, as well as garbage collection.

[104] 24 C.F.R. 965.506 and 24 C.F.R. 5.632

[105] 24 C.F.R. 960.259 and 24 C.F.R. 966.4(c)

[106] 24 C.F.R. 960 Subpart F

[107] Some PHAs participating in the MTW demonstration program (described later in this report) have adopted time limit policies for public housing residents.

[108] PHAs are not permitted to evict families solely for being "over-income" if they are participating in the Family Self Sufficiency program or are receiving the earned income disregard (24 C.F.R. 960.261).

[109] Termination of tenancy does not necessarily mean eviction in all cases. A unit may be considered unassisted while it is occupied by an ineligible family.

[110] 42 U.S.C. 1437n(f).

[111] See HUD Notice PIH 2009-35(HA), "State Lifetime Sex Offender Registration," issued September 9, 2009.

[112] The concept of "no fault" eviction was litigated up to the Supreme Court, which ultimately ruled in favor of the policy. For more information, see CRS Report RS21199, *No-fault Eviction of Public Housing Tenants for Illegal Drug Use: A Legal Analysis of Department of Housing and Urban Development v. Rucker*.

[113] 24 C.F.R. Part 966, Subpart B

[114] In some years, FSS is funded within ROSS, in other years, it is funded separately.

[115] Some PHAs received a renewable grant for elderly disabled service coordinator funding in 1995 and the renewal of that funding has not been built into their annual funding from HUD, called the Elderly Disabled Service Coordinator program.

[116] The Section 3 requirement is governed by interim regulations, which can be found at 24 C.F.R. 135 et. seq.

[117] The modern public housing homeownership guidelines were established by the 1998 reform act. Public housing homeownership is governed by Section 32 of the U.S. Housing Act of 1937, as amended. Additional HUD guidance can be found at 24 C.F.R. 906 and HUD's Section 32 Desk Guide, which can be found on HUD's website at http://www.hud.gov/offices/pih/centers/sac/homeownership/section32deskguide.pdf.

[118] QHWRA (P.L. 105-276) authorized a demonstration program similar to MTW, called the Home Rule Grant Demonstration. Under it, up to 100 local jurisdictions were permitted to take over management of public housing with increased flexibility and given the ability to mix capital funds, operating funds, and voucher funds. A notice inviting communities to submit proposals was published in the *Federal Register*; however, no communities applied so the demonstration was never implemented.

[119] Over the years, additional agencies have been added at the direction of Congress.

[120] For more information on Moving to Work (MTW), see *Housing Agency Responses to Federal Deregulation: An Assessment of HUD's "Moving to Work" Demonstration*, Urban Institute, 2004.

[121] Each year, HUD's Congressional Budget Justifications provide an estimate of the number of units that were eligible to receive federal payments. That document indicates that in FY2009, there were 1.14 million public housing units eligible for payment. HUD also publishes an annual report on the public housing operating fund. In that report, HUD estimates that 1.18 million public housing units were under contract in CY2009, but only about 1.12 million were eligible for payments from the operating fund.

[122] The Center on Budget and Policy Priorities (CBPP) attempted to count the number of units available for occupancy in June 2008 by adjusting data from 2000 for estimates of units removed from the stock and those replaced and then excluding those units that are planned for demolition or disposition. They counted 1.16 million public housing units in 13,926 projects.

[123] The peak in public housing units available for occupancy came well after the peak in reservations for new units of public housing, given the long development periods for many projects.

[124] As noted earlier, P.L. 105-276 prohibits PHAs from using federal funding to create net new units of public housing. Since the time that provision was enacted, there has been one exception: the FY2009 economic stimulus act (P.L. 111-5) permitted the construction and acquisition of new units of public housing with the funding it provided.

[125] U.S. Department of Housing and Urban Development (HUD), http://www.hud.gov/offices/pih/centers/sac/ demo_dispo/.

[126] At the time this analysis was completed, unit-level data were not readily available.

[127] The poverty guidelines are issued annually by the U.S. Department of Health and Human Services (HHS) and are a simplified version of the poverty thresholds developed by the Census Bureau for statistical purposes. The poverty guidelines are used for administrative purposes such as determining financial eligibility for certain federal programs. The poverty guidelines are used for this discussion for the sake of simplicity. The full set of guidelines can be accessed at http://aspe.hhs.gov/poverty/08poverty.shtml.

[128] The two-person threshold was chosen for comparison because the median household size in the public housing program is two.

[129] The three-person threshold was chosen for comparison because the median household size of non-elderly, non-disabled families with children in the public housing program is three.

[130] Fair Market Rents (FMRs) are calculated annually by HUD for each metropolitan area and county in the country. They are meant to represent the cost of modest housing in the community. While not a perfect proxy for the actual market costs that a family may face, they are a useful measure and are often used as a proxy for local market rents.

[131] This type of point-in-time analysis has limitations. While it shows the makeup of the current population of recipients (the majority of whom have lived in public housing less than five years; and a sizeable minority of whom have lived in public housing for 20 or more years), it does not answer the question of how long a person entering public housing is likely to stay. That type of analysis requires longitudinal data, which are not readily available.

[132] U.S. Department of Housing and Urban Development (HUD), Office of Public and Indian Housing, Real Estate Assessment Center, Financial Management Division, *Operating Fund Annual Report CY2009*, February 24, 2010.

[133] U.S. Department of Housing and Urban Development (HUD), Office of Public and Indian Housing, Real Estate Assessment Center, Financial Management Division, *Explanation of Final Obligations under Public Housing Operating Fund Program for Calendar Year (CY) 2010*, updated November 1, 2010.

[134] President's FY2011 Budget Appendix, pp. 587-588.

[135] See HUD's FY2002 Congressional Budget Justifications, http://archives.hud.gov/budget/ fy02/cjs/part_1/ drugelimin.pdf.

[136] 24 C.F.R. Part 905.

[137] This language is taken from HUD's website, http://www.hud.gov/offices/pih/programs/ph/ capfund/index.cfm. To date, a final regulation governing use of capital fund dollars has not been published. Instead, PHAs are to use prior guidance related to public housing modernization and development at 24 C.F.R. 940 and 24 C.F.R. 970.

[138] Section 519 of P.L. 105-276.

[139] In FY2008, Congress directed HUD to complete a new capital needs assessment of public housing. That assessment was underway, but results were not yet available at the time this report was published.

[140] Meryl Finkel, Donna DeMarco, Hin-Kin (Ken) Lam, and Karen Rich, "Formula Capital Study: Capital Needs of the Public Housing Stock in 1998," prepared for the U.S. Department of Housing and Urban Development (HUD), 2000.

[141] With the exception of the one-time appropriation of $4 billion for public housing capital needs provided by the American Recovery and Reinvestment Act of 2009 (ARRA; P.L. 111-5).

[142] Division K of the Consolidated Appropriations Act, 2008, Committee Print of the House Committee on Appropriations on H.R. 2764 / P.L. 110-161.

[143] U.S. Department of Housing and Urban Development (HUD), http://www.hud.gov/offices/pih/programs/ph/ capfund/cffp.cfm.

[144] HUD published a proposed rule governing the Capital Fund Financing Program, as well as an Operating Fund Financing Program, U.S. Department of Housing and Urban Development (HUD), "Use of Public Housing Capital and Operating Funds for Financing Activities," 72 *Federal Register* 39546, July 18, 2007. To date, a final rule has not been published. HUD has also published on its website a Notice for Comment on a proposed public housing mortgage program at http://www.hud.gov/offices/pih/programs/ph/capfund/prop-phmp-notice.pdf.

[145] As discussed in the notes accompanying Figure 6 and Table 7, a change in the way operating funds were provided to PHAs in FY2005 led to appropriations savings without commensurate reductions in the overall program level. Therefore, the dip in per unit appropriations in FY2005 should not be regarded as a decrease in funding available per unit.

[146] A modified version of PETRA was introduced shortly before the adjournment of the 111th Congress (H.R. 6468).

[147] Excluding the ARRA funding provided in FY2009, the average annual funding per unit eligible for payment provided for public housing has been at or under about $6,000 per year, as shown in Figure 6. According to HUD's FY2011 Congressional Budget Justifications (p. J-10), the average annual per voucher cost (not including administrative costs) has been above $6,000 per year since FY2004 and is currently over $7,000.

In: Public Housing: Background and Issues ISBN: 978-1-61324-778-5
Editor: Sara M. Larsen

Chapter 2

PUBLIC HOUSING: FACT SHEET ON THE OPERATING FUND FORMULA*

Maggie McCarty

SUMMARY

The local public housing authorities (PHAs) that administer the federal public housing program began receiving their annual federal operating subsidies under a new formula in January 2007. As a result of this formula change, some PHAs were eligible for an increase in their eligibility for funding and others were eligible for a decrease. Both the increases and the decreases were phased in (over two and five years, respectively) and PHAs that faced declines were eligible to limit their losses by adopting management reforms—which were also a part of the new operating fund requirements—earlier than required.

Since the formula is only used to determine eligibility for funding, the amount that a PHA qualifies for under the formula (whether it is an increase or a decrease) will be reduced if Congress appropriates less money than is necessary to fund all agencies at 100% of their eligibility, which it has done in the past.

---

* This is an edited, reformatted and augmented version of a Congressional Research Service publication, CRS Report for Congress RS22557, from www.crs.gov, dated January 7, 2011.

Introduction

The federal government supplies subsidies to PHAs to help make up the difference between what low-income tenants pay in rent and the cost of operating low-rent public housing. The formula for providing these operating funds changed in January 2007. Under the formula change, some PHAs were eligible to receive an increase in federal operating funds compared to the previous formula, and others qualified for a decrease. Both the increases and the decreases are phased in; PHAs facing decreases had an opportunity to limit their formula eligibility losses through the adoption of management changes. However, the amount that a PHA qualifies for under the new operating fund formula (whether it is an increase or a decrease) is reduced if Congress appropriates less money than is necessary to fund all agencies at 100% of their eligibility (as Congress has done in most recent years). This report is designed to provide a brief overview of the changes to the public housing operating fund formula that began in January 2007.

Background

Public housing costs are divided into two main categories: capital costs and operating costs. Capital costs are the costs of major renovations or modernizations. Operating costs are the day-to-day costs of running a building, such as utility, administrative, and routine maintenance costs. Operating costs vary based on many factors, including the age of a building, its heating and cooling systems, and its location. In the early years of the public housing program, PHAs were expected to meet their operating costs through the rents they collected. Over time, tenant rents were no longer sufficient to cover public housing operating expenses, in part because tenants became poorer and therefore unable to pay as much in rent, and in part because the costs of maintaining the buildings increased as they aged. In the late 1960s, Congress began providing operating subsidies to PHAs to supplement the low rents paid by tenants.

The system in place for providing those subsidies until 2001 was the Performance Funding System (PFS). In a 1998 public housing reform law, Congress responded to criticisms that the PFS formula was outdated by creating a new Public Housing Operating Fund.[1] The law required the Department of Housing and Urban Development (HUD) to use negotiated rulemaking to develop a new formula for distributing the funds. A negotiated rulemaking committee convened in 1999 involved PHAs and other stakeholder groups. During deliberation, it was agreed that sufficient data were not available to determine the true costs of operating public housing and that a study should be undertaken.[2] Until the results of the study were available, the committee agreed to use a modified version of the PFS to create an interim operating fund formula. This interim formula took effect in 2001.[3] HUD contracted with the Harvard Graduate School of Design to conduct the public housing operating cost study; its results were published in 2003.[4] Another negotiated rulemaking committee was established to use the results of the study to develop a final formula to replace the interim formula. HUD published a proposed rule in the spring of 2005,[5] but the rule was criticized for differing significantly from the agreements made during negotiated rulemaking. HUD published a final rule in the fall of 2005 that more closely resembled the initial agreement of the negotiated rulemaking committee.[6] The new formula took effect in January 2007. PHAs, which are funded on a calendar year basis, began receiving funding under the new formula in CY2007.[7]

Operating Fund Formula

The operating fund provides subsidies to PHAs to make up the difference between what it costs to run public housing and what low-income tenants pay in rent. Under the interim formula, the calculation for determining a PHA's operating subsidy eligibility used two components: formula expenses (meant to represent the cost of running public housing) and formula income (meant to represent the amount collected in tenant rents). HUD subtracts a PHA's formula income from its formula expenses and the amount by which the income is short of the expenses is the PHA's operating subsidy eligibility. The new operating fund formula uses the same principle, but a more complex equation with changes to the way certain components are calculated.

Formula Expenses

Formula expenses are the sum of three categories of estimated expenses: non-utility expenses, utility expenses, and other add-ons.

Non-Utility Project Expense Levels

Non-utility expense levels are per unit estimates of the basic non-utility operating costs of maintaining public housing.[8] Under the old formula, the non-utility expense levels set for a PHA were called Allowable Expense Levels (AELs). They were set for most PHAs under the PFS in 1975 and subsequently updated for inflation. The AELs were modified in 1992 and again in 2001 when the interim rule was adopted.[9] To calculate the non-utility expense component of a PHA's formula expenses under the interim operating fund formula, the number of public housing units in a PHA's inventory[10] was multiplied by the agency's AEL.

The new operating fund formula sets new non-utility expense levels for PHAs based on the data from the Harvard study and adjusted for inflation. These new *project* expense levels (PELs) are not applied at the agency level (as under the interim rule), rather, they differ for each project within a PHA's portfolio based on the characteristics of that project.[11] To calculate the non-utility expense component of a PHA's formula expenses under the new operating fund formula, the number of eligible public housing units[12] in each project in a PHA's inventory is multiplied by each project's PEL and those amounts are then summed.[13] For the CY2007 funding cycle, HUD developed weighted average project expense levels (WAPELs) for each PHA, and applied the WAPEL to all PHA units; for CY2008 and beyond, HUD has used individual PELs.

Utility Expense Levels

Utility expense levels (UELs) are estimates of the utility costs that can be attributed to a unit of public housing. They are calculated for each utility based on a PHA's consumption level and the applicable rates for that utility. The interim formula had aspects designed to encourage PHAs to adopt more energy-efficient practices and reduce consumption. The Harvard Cost Study did not make recommendations for changing utility expense levels, citing a lack of available data.[14] The final rule largely maintains the existing formula for calculating UELs, although the rule does state that HUD will study options for calculating utility costs and will convene a negotiated rulemaking committee to come up with a new formula.[15]

Add-Ons

In addition to basic utility and non-utility expenses, the interim operating fund formula included some add-on costs that PHAs could qualify to include in their formula expenses. Some of these add-ons were flat per-unit per-month or per-unit per-year fees; others were open-ended reimbursements. The new operating fund formula includes several new add-ons, including the reasonable cost of a self sufficiency program; an asset management fee for PHAs in compliance with asset management requirements ($4 per unit per month for PHAs with more than 250 units and $2 per unit per month for PHAs with 250 units or less); information technology fees ($2 per unit per month); asset repositioning fees (for units being removed from the public housing stock that are not eligible for operating funds); reasonable costs for energy conservation measures; and payment in lieu of taxes (PILOT) costs (which were included in the AELs under the old formula).[16]

Formula Income

Formula income represents the income a PHA collects from rents. Under the interim rule, formula income was calculated by computing a PHA's average monthly rental charge per unit, applying an upward trend factor, and multiplying it by the number of units expected to be occupied.[17] Under the new operating fund rule, formula income was initially calculated by taking the average rent charged by each PHA in its 2004 fiscal year and multiplying it by the PHA's eligible units.[18] Each PHA's formula income was frozen at this 2004 level through the CY2009 funding cycle.[19] Because tenants in public housing pay an income-based rent, as their incomes rise, so does the amount they pay in rent. With formula income frozen at the 2004 level, PHAs were provided an incentive to encourage families to increase their incomes, as the increased revenue from rents was not used when calculating a PHA's operating fund eligibility until after 2009. According to HUD, "unfreezing" income in 2010 resulted in the accounting for an additional $400 million in rental income over 2009.[20]

PHASE-IN

Under the new formula, some PHAs were "gainers," meaning that they were eligible for an increase in funding under the new formula as compared to the amount of funding they would have received under the old formula. Others were "decliners," meaning that they qualified for less funding under the new formula then they would have if the old formula had been maintained. A HUD analysis found that 74% of PHAs would have qualified for higher funding if the new operating fund formula had been in place in 2004; 26% of PHAs would have qualified for less funding.[21] To help ease the transition, losses will be phased in over five years; gains were phased in over two years (see Table 1 for the phase-in schedule). To implement the phase-in, HUD calculated a transition amount for each PHA. The transition amount was the difference between a PHA's operating subsidy eligibility in 2004 and what the PHA's eligibility would have been if the new formula had been in effect. The transition amount for each PHA was adjusted by each year's phase-in level and then either added to or subtracted from each PHA's operating subsidy eligibility level for that year.

For example, if a PHA's operating subsidy eligibility was $500,000 in 2004 but would have been only $450,000 if the new formula had been in place, the PHA would be considered a decliner, and its transition amount would be $50,000. Under the phase-in schedule, declines are limited to 5% in the first year, and so $47,500 (50,000 x 95%), would have been *added* to the PHA's 2007 operating subsidy eligibility. If the situation were reversed and the PHA would have gone from $450,000 under the old formula to $500,000 under the new formula, the PHA would be considered a gainer. Its transition amount would still be $50,000, but since gains are limited to 50% in the first year, $25,000 would have been *subtracted* from the PHA's 2007 operating subsidy eligibility.

Table 1. Phase-In Rates for Operating Subsidy Transition Funding

Year	Phase-In for Declines	Phase-In for Gains
1 (2007)	-5%	50%
2 (2008)	-24%	100%
3 (2009)	-43%	100%
4 (2010)	-62%	100%
5 (2011)	-81%	100%
6 (2012)	-100%	100%

Source: HUD, "Public Housing Operating Fund Program; Revised Transition Funding Schedule for FY2008 Through FY2012: Proposed Rule," 71 Federal Register 68404, November 24, 2006.

PHAs wishing to limit their losses can transition to asset-based management before the 2011 deadline (discussed below).[22] PHAs that transition to asset-based management in the preceding year stopped their losses for the following year and thereafter at that year's phase-in rate.[23] For example, a PHA that adopted asset-based management by the deadline in the first year would have limited its losses to 5%, meaning that HUD will add 95% of its transition amount to its operating subsidy eligibility each year.

Asset-Based Management[24]

One major recommendation of the Harvard study was that PHAs should transition to asset-based management. In the past, PHAs budgeted and were funded on an agency-wide basis, rather than on a project-by-project basis. They were also permitted to manage all of their units from a central office. This system differed from private market multifamily housing norms, where each property is treated as an individual asset and managed on an individual basis. In the final operating fund rule, HUD directed PHAs to adopt project-based budgeting and project-based accounting by PHA FY2007, and project-based management by PHA FY2011.[25]

OPERATING SUBSIDY FUNDING

The amount of operating subsidy a PHA is *eligible* to receive is not necessarily the amount of funding it will *actually* receive. The amount of funding appropriated by Congress for the operating fund is generally less than the amount necessary to fund all PHAs at 100% of their eligibility. As a result, HUD must apply an across-the-board cut to PHAs' operating subsidy levels in order to stay within the amount appropriated by Congress. The percentage of formula eligibility PHAs receive after the across-the-board cut is referred to as the proration level. As shown in Table 2, for several years proration levels were declining, meaning that PHAs were receiving a smaller and smaller share of the total funding for which they are eligible. Proration levels began increasing in recent years and reached over 100% in CY2010. The substantial increase in proration in CY2010 appears to be due, in part, to the effect of "unfreezing" formula income, which accounted for an additional $400 million in formula eligibility that did not have to be met through subsidy. Without the "unfreezing" of formula income, the proration level in CY2010 would have been about 94%.

The Harvard Operating Cost study found that, on the whole, the government has been under-funding the operating costs of PHAs. HUD's own transition analysis indicated that if the new formula had been in place in 2004, PHAs would have been eligible for an additional $264 million. That means that if the new formula had been in place in 2004, with the same appropriations level, the proration level for 2004 would have been lower (and PHAs would have received less than 98% of their funding eligibility).

Table 2. Operating Fund Prorations, 1998-2010

Year	Appropriation (in millions of nominal $)	Proration (%)
2010	4,760[a]	103.0
2009	4,455	88.4
2008	4,200	89.0
2007	3,864	83.4
2006	3,564	86.0
2005[b]	2,437	88.8
2004	3,579	98.1
2003	3,577	94.7
2002	3,495	100.0
2001	3,235	99.5
2000	3,138	98.5
1999	2,818	92.5
1998	2,900	100.0

Source: Table prepared by CRS. Appropriation figures are taken from the Office of Management and Budget's public budget database; proration levels are taken from data available on HUD's website: http://www.hud.gov/offices/pih/programs/ph/am/of/prorationlevels.pdf, http://www.hud.gov/offices/pih/programs/ph/am/of/2006prorationexpl_sept06.pdf http://www.hud.gov/offices/pih/programs/ph/am/of/2007prorationexplfnl.pdf, http://www.hud.gov/offices/pih/programs/ph/am/of/2008fnlprrtnexplntn.pdf, http://www.hud.gov/offices/pih/ programs/ph/am/of/opfund-report-09.pdf, and http://www.hud.gov/offices/pih/programs/ph/am/of/2010expln-octoblig.pdf.

[a] Excludes $15 million transfer to the Transformation Initiative.

[b] In 2005, Congress approved a budgeting change that led to a one-time appropriations savings, without a corresponding decrease in the program level. The comparable program level was $3,396 million.

The Harvard Operating Cost study found that, on the whole, the government has been underfunding the operating costs of PHAs. HUD's own transition analysis indicated that if the new formula had been in place in 2004, PHAs would have been eligible for an additional $264 million. That means that if the new formula had been in place in 2004, with the same appropriations level, the proration level for 2004 would have been lower (and PHAs would have received less than 98% of their funding eligibility).

End Notes

[1] Sec. 519, Quality Housing and Work Opportunity Responsibility Act 1998 (P.L. 105-276).

[2] HUD, "Revisions to the Public Housing Operating Fund Program: Final Rule," 79 *Federal Register* 54984, September 19, 2005. (Hereinafter referred to as "Final Rule.") See preamble.

[3] HUD, "Allocation of *Operating* Subsides under the Operating Fund Formula," 66 *Federal Register* 17276, March 29, 2001. (Hereinafter referred to as "Interim Rule.")

[4] Harvard University Graduate School of Design, Public Housing Operating Cost Study: Final Report, June 16, 2003.

[5] HUD, "Revisions to the Public Housing Operating Fund Program; Proposed Rule," 70 *Federal Register* 19858, April 14, 2005. (Hereinafter referred to as "Proposed Rule.")

[6] The Final Rule replaces the existing 24 CFR Part 990 et. seq.

[7] The rule initially scheduled implementation for 2006, but implementation was delayed by the HUD notice "Revisions to the Public Housing Operating Fund Program; Correction to Formula Implementation Date," 70 *Federal Register* 61366, October 24, 2005.

[8] Examples of non-utility operating costs include administrative costs (advertising the availability of units, processing of applications), safety and security costs, and routine maintenance.

[9] See Interim Rule, 24 CFR 990.105.

[10] Eligible units were units available for occupancy; long term vacancies and vacancies above 3% are not considered eligible for occupancy. See Interim Rule, 24 CFR 990.102.

[11] Projects are not necessarily individual buildings. Rather, they are groupings of units established by PHAs under 24 CFR 990.665, Final Rule.

[12] Eligible units are occupied units, units with an approved vacancy, and other vacant units (not to exceed 3% of the PHAs inventory). See 24 CFR 990.125, Final Rule.

[13] See 24 CFR 990.165, Final Rule.

[14] Harvard Graduate School of Design, *Benchmarking Public Housing Utility Funding to Private Norms: A Feasibility Study* (DRAFT), March 22, 2002.

[15] See 24 CFR 990.170-185, Final Rule.

[16] See 24 CFR 990.190, Final Rule. For former add-ons, see Interim Rule, 24 CFR 990.108.

[17] See Interim Rule, 24 CFR 990.109.

[18] See 24 CFR 990.195, Final Rule.

[19] A PHA can appeal to have its formula income adjusted if it can show that a severe local economic hardship is affecting its ability to maintain "some semblance" of its formula income.

[20] HUD, *Fiscal Year 2011 Budget Justification for Estimates*,pg. L-16, available at http://hud.gov/offices/cfo/reports/2011/cjs/public-housing-of2011.pdf.

[21] HUD, *New Operating Fund Formula Rule, Transition Analysis Report*, available at http://www.hud.gov/offices/pih/programs/ph/am/of/transitionanalys.xls.

[22] See HUD, "Public Housing Operating Fund Program; Revised Transition Funding Provision for Federal Fiscal Year 2007; Proposed Rule," 71 *Federal Register* 68408, November 24, 2006.

[23] Initially, HUD stated that PHAs were required to comply before April 15, 2007 to limit their losses to 5% in the first year (HUD Notice PIH 2006-35). HUD later stated that it would extend the deadline to October 15, 2007, for the first year. In the second year, PHAs will have to comply by April 15, 2008, if they wish to stop their losses at 24%. In the third year, PHAs wishing to stop their losses by 43% will have to comply by October 15, 2008.

[24] See 24 CFR 990 Subpart H, Final Rule.

[25] Under the Operating Fund rule, PHAs with fewer than 250 public housing units can choose to be exempt from the asset management requirement (unless they have been approved for stop-loss). Congress, in each annual appropriations act since FY2008, has expanded the threshold to agencies with 400 or fewer units.

In: Public Housing: Background and Issues ISBN: 978-1-61324-778-5
Editor: Sara M. Larsen

Chapter 3

HOPE VI PUBLIC HOUSING REVITALIZATION PROGRAM: BACKGROUND, FUNDING, AND ISSUES*

Maggie McCarty

SUMMARY

The Revitalization of Distressed Public Housing program, referred to as HOPE VI, has been credited with eliminating and replacing some of the most dangerous and dilapidated public housing in the country with new mixed income communities. However, the program has come under scrutiny for slow expenditure of funds and for displacing poor families. Reflecting these criticisms, the Bush Administration requested no new funding for the program in each budget request from FY2004-FY2009, and the Obama Administration requested no new funding (proposing, instead, that Congress fund a new program) in the FY2010 and FY2011 budget requests. Congress responded by continuing to fund the program, but at less than a quarter of what it had been funded at in FY2003 and prior years.

Created in 1992 and administered by the Department of Housing and Urban Development (HUD), the HOPE VI program provides funds to renovate or demolish existing public housing and replace it with mixed-

* This is an edited, reformatted and augmented version of a Congressional Research Service publication, dated CRS Report for Congress RL32236, from www.crs.gov, dated January 7, 2011.

income housing. The local public housing authorities (PHAs) that administer public housing apply for grants and use the funds to leverage other private and public resources. The main component of the HOPE VI program is revitalization grants, which can be used for demolition, rehabilitation, and new construction of public housing, as well as land acquisition, relocation of residents, and community and supportive services for residents. HUD has also provided demolition-only grants that could be used—often in conjunction with revitalization grants—for the physical destruction of distressed public housing and the relocation of its residents, although no demolition grants have been issued for several years. A third type of grant, planning grants, are no longer awarded, but could be used for technical assistance in preparing a property to go through a demolition or revitalization. Another type of revitalization grant, Main Street Revitalization Grants, was created in 2003. They are available to local governments in small communities rather than PHAs for main street revitalization projects, which may be unrelated to public housing.

Over the history of the program, 268 HOPE VI revitalization grants (incluing Main Street grants) have been made to PHAs in 41 states, districts, and territories. As of June 2009, the program had been responsible for the demolition of 93,295 units of public housing and the construction or substantial rehabilitation of 78,692 replacement units.

The HOPE VI program has helped transform a number of severely distressed neighborhoods, which has made the program popular with many members of Congress from both parties. The program's authorization was set to expire at the end of FY2006, but Congress has extended the authorization for the program each year in the annual appropraitions acts.

Beginning with its FY2010 budget request to Congress, the Obama Administration has requested that Congress replace the HOPE VI program with a new program, the Choice Neighborhoods Initiative (CNI), which would expand the scope of HOPE VI beyond public housing to other assisted housing, with a greater focus on neighborhood revitalization. The House Financial Services approved authorizing legislation in the 111th Congress (H.R. 5814), but it was not enacted before the end of the session. Congress did fund a demonstration of CNI in the FY2010 HUD appropriations act.

This report outlines the program and its history, which sets the context for today's debate.

Introduction

HOPE VI is a public housing reform program. Through HOPE VI, the Department of Housing and Urban Development (HUD) provides funds to rehabilitate or demolish public housing and replace it with housing that serves both the poor as well as the middle class. In order to understand HOPE VI and its issues, it is important to first understand a brief history of the larger public housing program.

History of Public Housing

The Low-Rent Public Housing program was created as a part of the U.S. Housing Act of 1937 (P.L. 75-412). The Depression-era program was intended to stimulate construction activity, clear slums, and provide low-rent housing to poor families. As designed under the act, public housing is built and operated by local, quasi-governmental, public housing authorities (PHAs). Tenants who live in public housing typically pay 30% of their adjusted gross incomes toward rent, although they can opt for a market-based flat rent and PHAs can choose to institute minimum rents of up to $50 per month. PHAs are able to keep public housing rents low because local governments provide property tax reductions and the federal government provides both capital and operating subsidies to supplement the low rents paid by tenants.

From its inception, public housing has faced a number of barriers to success. Many communities were resistant to accepting public housing. This opposition, paired with strict federal rules about how much could be spent to build a unit of public housing, led to the construction of public housing developments in undesirable areas, such as near railroad tracks, highways, and industrial zones. The housing that was constructed was often high-density, high-rise structures. This form of development has often been characterized as "the projects." In addition to location and construction problems, many projects faced management problems. Although many public housing projects were run by effective and efficient PHAs, others had inexperienced PHAs, or in some cases, negligent PHAs, who were unable or unwilling to deal with problems as they arose.

Furthermore, PHA budgets were often insufficient to maintain the properties. It was thought at the time the program was created that most tenants would be working adults whose incomes would increase until their economic situation improved enough that they could move out of public housing. This was the case in the early years of the program. However, policies that adopted rent levels based on incomes rather than operating costs and gave priority to the elderly and disabled, paired with changing demographics and a growth in single-mother-headed households, resulted in a population of public housing residents that was very different than originally envisioned. Today, about half of public housing residents are elderly or disabled and about half are non-elderly, non-disabled single-adult-headed households, the majority with children. Of those non-elderly, non-disabled households, only about half have income from work, while the other half either receive some form of cash assistance, such as welfare, or report no income. Today's public housing serves the very poor, who are only required to pay a percentage of their income toward rent. Since the rent that PHAs receive from tenants is so low, public housing is dependent on congressional appropriations, and the budget has not always kept up with need. Many units of public housing fell into disrepair, and some units had to be left vacant because they were no longer habitable. Public housing, over time, became known for terrible living conditions. Research has shown that communities with high concentrations of poverty often fall victim to myriad social ills.[1] The often dense, high-rise structures of public housing became riddled with crime, drugs, and violence.

Public housing was the primary government housing program for the poor until the late 1970s. However, out of growing concern about the problems with public housing, and other government-subsidized housing construction programs, President Nixon declared a moratorium on federal housing construction programs in 1973. In 1974, Congress authorized the Section 8 program, which provided subsidies to allow low-income families to live in private market housing. It was hoped that through partnerships with the private sector, the Section 8 program could avoid the problems faced by public housing. The Section 8 program also introduced tenant-based assistance, which subsidized tenants rather than units, giving tenants the option to move. Tenant-based assistance has grown in popularity, partially out of the hope that it can prevent concentrations of poverty in neighborhoods. Over time, Section 8 overtook public housing as the government's largest housing program for the poor; today, almost twice as many households are served by Section 8 than are housed in public housing.[2]

Basis for HOPE VI

Although new construction of public housing had ended by the early 1970s, over 1 million units of public housing were still occupied, and many were still plagued by problems. In order to determine how to deal with the existing stock of public housing, Congress created the National Commission on Severely Distressed Public Housing (P.L. 101-235) in 1989. The commission was mandated to identify those public housing projects that were in a severe state of distress; assess the most promising strategies for improvement; and develop a national action plan.

In 1992, the commission issued its findings and recommendations on the state of the nation's public housing. The commission labeled 6% of the public housing stock as severely distressed, at the time, equal to 86,000 units. It also reported finding the following:

- residents afraid to move about in their own homes and communities because of the high incidence of crime;
- high unemployment and limited opportunities for the meaningful employment of residents;
- programs designed to address the conditions with too few resources, provided too late;
- programs designed to assist residents of public housing that provide disincentives to self-sufficiency; and
- families living in physical conditions that have deteriorated to a degree that renders the housing dangerous to the health and safety of residents.

The national action plan presented by the commission included proposals for change in five major categories:

- **Addressing the needs of residents**: recommendations included increasing funding for social services, increasing coordination among federal agencies that provide social services, and promoting economic development opportunities for residents.
- **Addressing the physical conditions**: recommendations included increasing funding for capital improvements, providing national leadership to PHAs in planning and design, establishing a model process to eliminate the causes of severe distress, and increasing

coordination among government programs that support the rehabilitation of severely distressed housing.

- **Addressing management needs**: recommendations included providing funding for security, further tying PHA funding to performance, and promoting income-mixing in public housing.
- **Other strategies**: recommendations included encouraging PHAs to pursue private and non-profit management opportunities, increasing and improving available data on public housing, creating a new office on severely distressed public housing at HUD, and encouraging Congress to authorize a new partnership program between PHAs, non-profits, the private sector, and residents to attract additional resources to public housing.

History of HOPE VI

HOPE VI began as a demonstration program, created in reaction to the findings of the National Commission on Severely Distressed Public Housing. The commission's National Action Plan was presented in August 1992; in October 1992 the final version of the FY1993 HUD appropriations bill (P.L. 102-389) passed Congress, including $300 million for an *Urban Revitalization Demonstration* program. Under the demonstration, the Secretary of HUD was to choose 15 cities,

based on need, to receive up to $50 million each to revitalize distressed public housing. Each city was required to spend 80% of its funds toward the capital costs of major reconstruction, rehabilitation and other physical improvements, the capital costs of replacement units and/or Section 8 certificates, management improvements for the reconstructed project, and for planning and technical assistance purposes. The remaining 20% was to be used for community and supportive services. PHAs were required to match 15% of all funds provided.

From 1993 until 1998, the Urban Revitalization Demonstration, now commonly referred to as HOPE VI, continued to receive funding through annual appropriations bills; however, the program remained unauthorized. The law governing the program was contained within annual appropriations bills and the requirements for eligibility and funding changed from year to year. HUD administered the law not through regulation, but in the directions it issued along with each annual Notice of Funding Availability (NOFA), to which communities would apply for HOPE VI funding. Changes to the program, in addition to those mandated by annual appropriations laws, were included in these NOFAs.

The FY1999 HUD appropriations bill (P.L. 105-276) included a major public housing reform initiative, the Quality Housing and Work Opportunity Reconciliation Act (QHWRA), that authorized the HOPE VI program. QHWRA codified four purposes for the program:

- improving the living environment for public housing residents of severely distressed public housing projects through the demolition, rehabilitation, reconfiguration, or replacement of obsolete public housing projects (or portions thereof);
- revitalizing sites (including remaining public housing dwelling units) on which such public housing projects are located and contributing to the improvement of the surrounding neighborhood;
- providing housing that will avoid or decrease the concentration of very low-income families; and
- building sustainable communities.[3]

In the law, severely distressed public housing was defined as public housing that

- requires major redesign, reconstruction or redevelopment, or partial or total demolition;
- is a significant contributing factor to the physical decline of and disinvestment by public and private entities in the surrounding neighborhood;
- is occupied predominantly by families that are very low-income families with children, unemployed, and dependent on various forms of public assistance; or has high rates of vandalism and criminal activity (including drug-related criminal activity) in comparison to other housing in the area;
- cannot be revitalized through assistance under other programs because of cost constraints and inadequacy of available amounts; and
- is lacking in sufficient appropriate transportation, supportive services, economic opportunity, schools, civic and religious institutions, and public services, resulting in severe social distress in the project.[4]

QHWRA authorized funding for HOPE VI through the end of FY2002 and included a sunset clause which stated that no assistance could be provided to the program after September 30, 2002. The FY2003 HUD appropriations bill (P.L. 108-7) extended authorization for the HOPE VI program through the end of FY2004 and P.L. 108-186 reauthorized the program, with some changes, through FY2006. Each year since, Congress has extended the program's authorization in the annual appropriations acts.[5] The program lacks formal regulation; guidance is set out for each cohort of grantees in the annual Notice of Funding Availability to which they apply for funds.

THE PROGRAM

The purpose of the HOPE VI program is to revitalize severely distressed public housing developments and transform them into safe, liveable environments. As described by HUD, this includes

- changing the physical characteristics of public housing from high-rise tenements to attractive, marketable units that blend in with the surrounding neighborhoods;
- lessening concentrations of poverty by reducing density and promoting mixed-income communities;
- encouraging partnerships with other agencies and local governments for support and resources; achieving high-quality management in public housing and enforcing strict eviction rules; and
- helping residents to attain self-sufficiency by providing services and educational opportunities, and by encouraging economic development in the area surrounding public housing.

HUD seeks to meet the goals of the HOPE VI program by providing grants to PHAs for revitalization, or if this is not economically feasible, for demolition of distressed public housing. The majority of funds are awarded through revitalization grants; funds have also been awarded through demolition grants (until FY2004) and planning grants (until FY1995). A 2003 HOPE VI reauthorization law (P.L. 108-186) created a fourth type of HOPE VI grant, designed to promote "main street" revitalization in small communities, which is unrelated to public housing.

HOPE VI Funding and Grants

Funding for the HOPE VI program increased in the beginning, but remained relatively steady over many years. However, in the face of mounting budget pressures and a desire from the Bush Administration to eliminate funding for the program (discussed later in this report), Congress enacted a major decrease in funding in FY2004 that has been continued each year since. Table 1 presents HOPE VI appropriations from FY1993 to FY2010.

Table 1. HOPE VI Appropriations, FY1993-FY2010 (dollars in millions)

FY	Public Law	Appropriations
1993	P.L. 102-389	$300
1994	P.L. 103-124	778
1995	P.L. 103-327	500
1996	P.L. 104-134	480
1997	P.L. 104-204	550
1998	P.L. 105-65	550
1999	P.L. 105-276	625
2000	P.L. 106-569	575
2001	P.L. 106-377	574
2002	P.L. 107-73	574
2003	P.L. 108-7	570
2004	P.L. 108-199	149
2005	P.L. 108-447	143
2006	P.L. 109-115	99
2007	P.L. 110-5	99
2008	P.L. 110-161	100
2009	P.L. 111-8	120
2010	P.L. 111-117	200[a]
Total		$6,986

Source: Table prepared by CRS using the United States Office of Management and Budget, Public Budget Database for FY1993-FY2007. FY2008-FY2010 figures taken from appropriations laws.

[a] Of this amount, $65 million is set aside for a new Choice Neighborhoods Demonstration, modeled after HOPE VI, but not limited to public housing (discussed later in this report).

This funding has been used to provide 587 grants. Table 2 shows the amount and number of grants awarded, by type, from FY1993 to FY2009.[6]

Table 2. HOPE VI Awards, FY1993-2009 (dollars in millions)

FY	Revitalization Grants		Other Grant Types							
			Main Street		Demolition-Only		Planning		Totals	
	$	#	$	#	$	#	$	#	$	#
1993	566	13	—	—	0	0	1	2	567	15
1994	516	14	—	—	0	0	3	6	519	20
1995	475	13	—	—	0	0	11	27	486	40
1996	383	19	—	—	71	22	—	—	454	41
1997	497	23	—	—	1	4	—	—	498	27
1998	532	28	—	—	52	46	—	—	584	74
1999	573	21	—	—	40	31	—	—	613	52
2000	514	18	—	—	52	27	—	—	566	45
2001	492	16	—	—	75	44	—	—	567	60
2002	492	27	—	—	42	41	—	—	534	68
2003	433	24	—	—	60	69	—	—	493	93
2004	127	7	2[a]	5	0	0	—	—	129	12
2005[b]	157	8	[c]	[c]	0	0	—	—	157	8
2006	72	4	1	1	0	0	—	—	73	5
2007	89	5	[d]	[d]	0	0	—	—	89	5
2008	97	6	4	4	0	0	—	—	97	10
2009	113	6	5	6	0	0	—	—	118	12
Total	6,128	252	10	16	393	284	15	35	6,544	587

Source: Congressional Research Service (CRS) analysis of HUD expenditure data and FY2004, FY2005, FY2006, FY2007, FY2008, and FY2009 grant award statements.

Note: As of the date of this report, FY2010 grant awards had not been announced.

[a] The FY2004 Main Street Revitalization Grants were awarded in FY2005.

[b] Does not include three “Mentoring Demonstration” grants, totaling $500,000, awarded in FY2005. These grants were created by the Secretary with previous year’s appropriations funding. See discussion under “Residents” heading later in this report.

[c] Note that FY2005 Main Street Grant funding was made available in combination with FY2006 Main Street Grant funding in the FY2006 Main Street Revitalization grants NOFA, published in the Federal Register on April 11, 2006.

[d] While $2 million was advertised as available for Main Street grants in FY2007, no funds appear to have been awarded.

Planning Grants

Thirty-five planning grants were awarded to PHAs between 1993 and 1995. They were used to pay for studies of the area to be revitalized; to develop a plan for revitalization; for economic development; and for technical support. Planning grants were suspended after 1995, because HUD believed that there were enough examples of PHAs that had begun the revitalizing process that the technical assistance was no longer necessary.

Demolition-Only Grants

In 1996, HUD established a goal of demolishing 100,000 units by the year 2003. Since then, the department has awarded 284 demolition-only grants. PHAs are awarded these grants when it is not economically feasible to redesign or reconstruct the existing units of a project. They are used to demolish existing units and to relocate the affected tenants in replacement housing, which could include providing them with tenant-based vouchers. Often, demolition-only grants are used as precursors to future HOPE VI revitalization grant initiatives. Since FY2004, when funding for HOPE VI was significantly reduced, HUD has not made any demolition-only grants available.

Main Street Revitalization Grants

The American Dream Downpayment Act (P.L. 108-186) added a new category of HOPE VI grants. Main Street Revitalization grants are awarded to units of local government (rather than PHAs) in small communities (with a population under 50,000) that are not currently served by a PHA, or are served by a small PHA (administer 100 or less units) and that have an active main street rejuvenation effort. Historically, the majority of HOPE VI grants have gone to large cities, arguably where the most blighted public housing is found. Funds can be used to develop affordable housing that is located in a community area that is undergoing a historic main street revitalization; there is no requirement that the use of funds be at all related to public housing. Main Street grants are statutorily capped at $1 million each (although HUD capped grants at $500,000 each in FY2005), and grantees must match at least 5% of the grant award. The grants are funded through a 5% set-aside in the HOPE VI annual appropriation. The first round of grants was made available in FY2004, but awarded in FY2005.

Revitalization Grants

The bulk of funding provided for the HOPE VI program has been awarded through revitalization grants,[7] which is the most well-known component of the program. HUD has awarded 246 revitalization grants since the inception of the HOPE VI program. They can be used for the development of new public housing, rehabilitation of existing public housing, demolition and/or disposition[8] of existing public housing, the creation of homeownership replacement units, the acquisition of new property, the relocation of displaced residents, community and supportive services for residents, and administrative fees and costs. Up to 20% of grant funds may be used for community and supportive services programs. Grantees must match grant funds, and they are generally used to leverage other resources.

Over the history of the HOPE VI program, over $6 billion worth of revitalization grants have been awarded to PHAs in 36 states and territories. In addition, $10 million in Main Street Revitalization grants have been awarded, including to five states which had never received HOPE VI Revitalization grants. Table 3 shows the breakdown of revitalization grants and awards by state.

Table 3. HOPE VI Revitalization and Main Street Revitalization Grants by State, FY1993-FY2009

State	Total Grants	Total Awards (in millions of $)
Alabama	6	119.7
Arizona	5	81.1
Arkansas[a]	1	0.9
California[b]	13	328.1
Colorado[b]	4	73.2
Connecticut	5	131.4
Delaware	1	16.8
District of Columbia	7	181.2
Florida	14	275.6
Georgia[b]	12	286.9
Illinois	13	367.6
Indiana	4	79.0
Iowa[b]	1	1.0
Kentucky	7	144.7
Louisiana[c]	6	116.5
Maine	1	1

State	Total Grants	Total Awards (in millions of $)
Maryland	9	209.8
Massachusetts	7	159.1
Michigan	4	127.6
Minnesota	2	34.2
Mississippi[c]	3	52.8
Missouri	7	172.4
Montana	1	0.9
New Jersey	16	417.1
New Mexico[a]	1	1.0
New York	7	197.5
North Carolina[a]	15	348.0
Ohio	12	313.9
Oklahoma	2	29.1
Oregon[c]	2	51.9
Pennsylvania	18	367.7
Puerto Ricoc[d]	3	51.2
Rhode Island[c]	2	20.5
South Carolina	7	146.5
South Dakota[e]	1	1.0
Tennesse[e]	12	301.8
Texas	13	373.5
Virginia	7	149.3
Washington	9	255.6
West Virginia	2	17.6
Wisconsin	6	136.5

Source: Congressional Research Service (CRS) analysis of HUD expenditure data through June 30, 2004, and HUD grant announcements for FY2004, FY2005, FY2006, FY2007, FY2008, and FY2009.

Note: As of the date of this report, FY2010 grant awards had not been announced.

[a] Includes one Main Street Grant totaling $869,000.

[b] Includes one Main Street Grant totaling $1 million.

[c] Includes one Main Street Grant totaling $500,000.

[d] Includes one Main Street Grant totaling $650,000.

[e] Includes one Main Street Grant totaling $977,500.

The Application and Awards Process

Each year, HUD publishes a NOFA in the *Federal Register* inviting PHAs to apply for HOPE VI grants. The NOFA includes application procedures and requirements, which change somewhat every year. PHAs submit applications requesting a specified amount of money to be used to implement a plan that they have detailed to HUD.

Demolition-Only Grants

Demolition-only grants were awarded on a first-come, first-served basis. Once the NOFA was published, eligible PHAs could apply. In order to be eligible, a PHA had to fall into one of four priority groups[9] that involve the mandatory or voluntary demolition of public housing or prior approval for a revitalization grant. HUD screened applications as they arrived to ensure that they were in a priority group and that they met minimum requirements. For example, in 2003, minimum requirements included a cap of 2,500 units to be demolished per applicant, a plan to relocate residents, and proof that the units are in severe distress. HUD funded eligible applicants on a first-come, first-served basis, by priority group, until the HOPE VI funds were exhausted. No demolition-only grants have been awarded since FY2003.

Main Street Grants

The application process for Main Street grants largely mirrors that for revitalization grants. A NOFA for Main Street grants is published in the Federal Register, laying out the application requirements and deadlines. Once HUD receives applications, it screens them to determine whether they meet threshold requirements. In the FY2009/FY2010 NOFA, the thresholds included requirements that the applicant had matching funding in place and leveraged funding available; that, if the applicant had received a prior award, adequate progress had been made; and that the applicant have a Main Street, among other requirements. Once applications have been screened, they are scored. Scoring categories in the FY2009/FY2010 NOFA included the capacity of the community, including prior experience, the need for affordable housing, the readiness of the plan for implementation, and the appropriateness of the plan. While Main Street grants are capped in law at $1 million, in some years HUD has limited the maximum to $500,000, presumably to serve more communities.

Revitalization Grants

PHAs that wish to receive a revitalization grant must apply by the deadline published in the NOFA. Once the deadline has passed, HUD screens the applications to ensure that they meet threshold requirements. If they do not, then they are disqualified. For example, in order to meet the threshold requirements in 2009, applicants had to prove, among other factors, that they had secured site control for the proposed site, had issued a Request for Qualifications (RFQ) to secure a developer, that they had prepared a plan in advance for relocating residents impacted by the revitalization, and that affected residents had been involved at the beginning and during the planning process. The NOFA also explains deadlines for spending funds and penalties for slow expenditure.

Once HUD screens the applications, the agency scores them on a variety of factors. For example, in the 2009 NOFA, applications received scores in categories including capacity to undertake development, need, the amount of outside resources brought in (leveraging), resident and community involvement, community and supportive services, commitment to early education, and the relocation plan. HUD then ranks the scored applications and funds them, in order, until the HOPE VI funds are exhausted. In the early years of the HOPE VI program, there was no cap on the amount a HOPE VI grantee could be awarded. However, since 1996, when HUD began allowing PHAs to use HOPE VI dollars to leverage outside resources, the average grant amount per project has dropped significantly. In recent years, HUD has generally capped revitalization grants at $20 million each, although in FY2009 several grants exceeded $20 million.

Once grantees are selected, they are notified and are required to sign a grant agreement with HUD. The grant agreement includes time-lines for progress. For example, under the terms of the 2009 NOFA, HOPE VI revitalization grantees are expected to complete their developments within 48-54 months. However, as the NOFAs change every year, different cohorts of grantees have had different time-lines for spending their funds. PHAs must agree to meet all requirements of the program, including match requirements. For example, PHAs must match 5% of their HOPE VI grant award with other resources and must match, dollar-for-dollar, any amount over 5% of the grant amount that is used for community and supportive services for residents. If a PHA is not successfully meeting its deadlines or requirements, HUD has the authority to penalize the PHA either by appointing some form of receiver or by rescinding grant funds. To date, HUD has not rescinded HOPE VI funds from delinquent grantees, although performance on a HOPE VI grant has contributed to HUD's finding of substantial default and appointment of a receiver for several PHAs.

Leveraging

One of the key components of the HOPE VI program is the leveraging of outside resources. Beginning in 1996, revitalization grantees were encouraged to seek outside sources of funding to undertake their redevelopment, in addition to meeting their match requirement. Since that time, grantees have partnered with private non-profit and for-profit organizations and local and state governmental entities who have contributed both expertise and resources to HOPE VI projects. In aggregate, PHAs have budgeted $2.16 in leveraged (meaning non-HOPE VI) funds for each HOPE VI revitalization grant dollar awarded. Figure 1 demonstrates the generally increasing trend in the amount of funds leveraged by HOPE VI grantees.

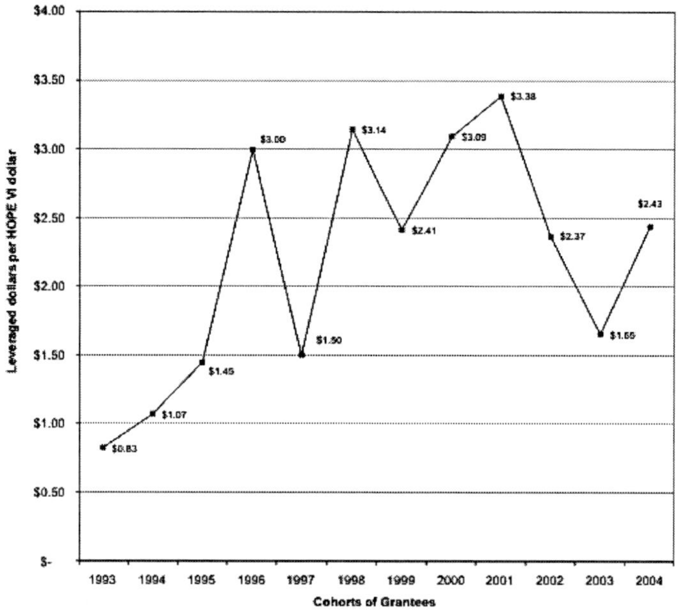

Source: CRS analysis of HOPE VI data (through March 31, 2006) from the U.S. Department of Housing and Urban Development, using the same methodology as used in U.S. General Accounting Office, GAO-03-91, *Hope VI Leveraging Has Increased, but HUD Has Not Met Annual Reporting Requirement,* November 2002, available at http://www.gao.gov/new.items/d0391.pdf.

Note: Numbers represent amount of leveraged resources budgeted to be spent relative to the amount of HOPE VI funding budgeted to be spent. Numbers do not reflect actual expenditures. Data are current as of March 2006.

Figure 1. HOPE VI Leveraging by Cohorts of Grantees.

Despite general satisfaction with the amount of non-HOPE VI funds grantees are bringing into projects, concern has been raised that HOPE VI redevelopments may be raising only limited private investment and may be more expensive than they appear. According to HUD's FY2006 HOPE VI Report to Congress, about 60% of funds spent on revitalization projects had come from leveraged funds, and 73% of those leveraged funds were from *non*-federal sources. However, that estimate includes private equity raised from the sale of Low-Income Housing Tax Credits (LIHTC) as a non-federal source, although some might consider it a form of federal funding. A study conducted by General Accounting Office (now the Government Accountability Office) in 2002 found that, after excluding LIHTC funds, only 12% of leveraged funds had come from private sources; LIHTC funding had accounted for 27% of all leveraged funds in the projects studied.[10]

SUCCESSES AND CONCERNS

HOPE VI has been credited with a number of successes. In terms of addressing severely distressed public housing, the program has largely met its original goal: to eliminate the worst severely distressed public housing. Grantees have been provided sufficient funding to demolish over 100,000 units of public housing.[11] The homes that are built in place of the demolished units are typically lower-density, safer, and more attractive. The new designs also generally connect the public housing developments with their surrounding communities, both functionally and aesthetically. Despite the HOPE VI program's successes, there are several issues in the program that have led some to call for reforms to the program. They include the slow expenditure of HOPE VI funds, the impact of HOPE VI on the original public housing residents, the cost-effectiveness of the program, and the loss of assisted housing stock.

Neighborhood Improvements

Success in the HOPE VI program can be measured, in part, by the amount of revitalization it has sparked in surrounding communities. Although this kind of change is hard to measure, studies have shown that HOPE VI has had some success. A study of eight HOPE VI sites undertaken by the Housing Research

Foundation found that in communities surrounding recent HOPE VI revitalization projects

- per capita incomes increased more than for the cities as a whole;
- neighborhood unemployment rates had fallen;
- receipt of public assistance had declined;
- fewer households qualified as low-income;
- commercial and residential lending rates increased at a faster rate than overall city increases; and
- overall and violent crime had declined at a more rapid rate than in the overall city.

The author concluded that "although there are many non-HOPE VI factors contributing to change in these communities, the nature of HOPE VI development has helped determine the extent and pace of that change."[12]

A 2003 GAO report looking at the neighborhoods surrounding several HOPE VI sites also attempted to assess the impact of HOPE VI on neighborhoods. Using decennial Census and Home Mortgage Disclosure Act data, GAO found that the neighborhoods surrounding the HOPE VI developments generally experienced positive changes in education, income, and housing indicators. However, further analysis found mixed results in some neighborhoods compared to comparable neighborhoods that had not undergone a HOPE VI redevelopment. In summary, GAO's report stated:

> We cannot attribute these changes solely to the HOPE VI program. To the extent that they do reflect the program's influence, however, they suggest that demolition of old, deteriorated public housing alone may influence surrounding neighborhoods. For example, average housing value and average household income increased even though no new units had been constructed. It is possible that the HOPE VI program influenced these indicators by removing blight from the neighborhoods and temporarily relocating large numbers of low-income households during demolition.[13]

Regardless of whether HOPE VI redevelopments actually spur new neighborhood improvement—or if such improvements would have happened without a HOPE VI grant—the award of a HOPE VI grant has often brought positive press to areas of towns that were plagued by negative perceptions. Many news stories have been written about community transformations linked to HOPE VI.[14] Arguably, HOPE VI might help to change the public's generally negative perceptions of public housing.

Mixed Finance

HOPE VI has encouraged PHAs to build relationships with outside partners, including nonprofits and the business community. These partnerships bring new resources into communities undergoing revitalization. Examples include the creation of community centers, charter schools, and new commercial activity in redeveloped HOPE VI sites and the provision of capital to help public housing residents start small businesses and social services to help public housing residents further their educations or overcome personal barriers.

PHAs have also gained new knowledge about private capital markets partly as a result of HOPE VI. This new knowledge has allowed a number of PHAs, outside of the HOPE VI program, to participate in mixed-finance deals and secure private loans. As of the end of FY2009, HUD has approved 116 transactions in which 200 PHAs secured a total of approximately $3.65 billion in loan and bond financing to address the capital needs of public housing.[15] These extra funds supplement federal funds and rents used to modernize public housing. It is hoped that, with the use of outside funding, PHAs can begin to address the large backlog of modernization needs in existing public housing and prevent further disrepair.

Residents

The majority of HOPE VI revitalization plans require at least the temporary displacement of residents. Grantees can relocate residents, either temporarily or permanently, to other public housing sites or by providing them with vouchers to be used in the private market. According to HUD program summary data, as of March 2006, 63,885 households had been relocated by HOPE VI revitalization grantees. Of those households, 49% had been moved to other public housing, 32% had been given Section 8 vouchers, 6% had been evicted, and 13% had made other arrangements or left the program. Of the 63,885 that were relocated, 22% are now living in revitalized units.

Although the intention of many grantees is to return as many displaced residents as possible to redeveloped sites, often fewer residents return than planned. GAO found that, in 1999, grantees estimated that 61% of original residents would return to redeveloped sites; by 2003, their estimate of resident returns had dropped to 44%.[16] Some families choose not to return, opting instead to stay where they were relocated and avoid the hassle of another move. In other cases, families are ineligible to move back because they do not meet additional screening requirements—sometimes related to criminal background or financial background (such as a history of unpaid rent)—adopted by the PHA for the project. According to March 2006 HUD data, grantees estimated that only 38% of original residents would return to redeveloped sites.

Given that many residents who are displaced from public housing projects undergoing HOPE VI renovation do not return or are not permitted to return when the revitalization is complete, low-income housing advocates have raised questions about what has happened to them. Since HUD has not always required PHAs to follow residents during the revitalization process, some PHAs have lost track of residents after their initial relocation. To learn more about what has happened to displaced residents, the Urban Institute conducted a study that looked at the living conditions of former residents of eight HOPE VI sites that had been relocated either with vouchers or to other public housing units, several years after their initial relocation. Their study found that, overall, relocated tenants lived in safer, healthier communities and better housing after relocation. Although both groups have seen some gains, families relocated with vouchers have generally fared better than families relocated to other public housing. Particularly, the study found that children in voucher households have done better than children relocated to other public housing, for whom behavior problems have increased. One way in which voucher holders have done worse includes financial hardship. Voucher holders are more likely than public housing residents to report difficulty in paying for utilities and food—indicating that they are having to make tradeoffs to pay their rent.[17] The Urban Institute also found that the most vulnerable and "hard to house" families struggled the most following a HOPE VI relocation, especially if they were relocated with vouchers.[18]

Low-income housing advocates argue that HUD should put a greater priority on the needs of public housing residents when selecting HOPE VI grantees. Advocates contend that more units of public housing should be built through HOPE VI and that displaced tenants should have a right to return. They also argue that PHAs should be responsible for providing sufficient support to displaced residents, especially residents that leave public housing and those that are most vulnerable, to ensure that their relocation is successful.

The Urban Institute findings have also led to calls for the greater use of vouchers when relocating families.[19]

Mentoring Demonstration Grants

In FY2005, HUD awarded more than $500,000 of prior years' funds for Mentoring Demonstration grants. They were awarded to prior revitalization grantees to partner with community and faith-based organizations who provide community and supportive services to families. HUD will use these grantees to see whether a "mentoring" model improves self-sufficiency outcomes for families affected by HOPE VI redevelopments. The grants were funded with previous years' appropriations funding, presumably recaptured from grantees who were unable to use them.

Expenditure

One of the major criticisms of the HOPE VI program in recent years has been the slow expenditure of HOPE VI funds. In FY2003, unspent balances reached a peak of over $3.3 billion (over half of the $6 billion appropriated for the program).

A number of reasons have been cited for PHAs' slow expenditure of HOPE VI funds. One is the changing nature of the program. In the beginning, grantees were chosen almost solely on the basis of need. Often, the PHAs with the most need had the weakest management capacity. As a result, the poorest-performing PHAs were awarded large grants. It is not surprising that they had difficulty in implementing their redevelopment plans. This was especially true in 1996, when Congress set aside grants for a set of PHAs outside of any competitive process.[20] A 2003 GAO report found that the majority of revitalization grantees had missed at least one of the deadlines established in their grant agreements.[21]

HUD has worked to address several of these problems. Over time, the process for selecting grantees has become more competitive, and HUD now uses a number of criteria to judge applicants' capacity for undertaking these complicated development projects. For example, recent revitalization NOFAs have included rating factors that reward applicant and developer capacity and deduct points from applicants with previous HOPE VI grants that are behind in development.

There is reason to believe that more recent HOPE VI grantees have performed better than earlier grantees. HUD's FY2006 2nd Quarter HOPE VI

Progress Report to Congress included information demonstrating the improved performance of more recent cohorts of grantees on a number of administrative performance measures. For example, the number of days it took more recent grantees (those from FY2002 through FY2004) from the execution of their grant agreement to the approval of their revitalization plan averaged 177 days, compared to an average of over 600 days for older grantees (those from FY1993 through FY2001). Pre-2002 grantees took an average of over 1,100 days to get approval of their mixed finance proposals, compared to an average of about 356 days for FY2002 and later grantees. These improvements may be due, in part, to more robust selection criteria used by HUD in choosing grantees, greater PHA experience and familiarity with HOPE VI-like mixed finance developments, and more focus by HUD on interim performance measures.

Another important change has come in the way that Congress provides funding to the HOPE VI program. Prior to FY2002, HOPE VI was provided with no-year funding, meaning that the funds provided by Congress remained available to the grantee until they were spent. Beginning in FY2002, Congress adopted a one-year obligation and a five-year expenditure deadline for HOPE VI funds. Any HOPE VI funds remaining unspent at the end of that period will expire and revert back to the Treasury. This change in funding should effectively solve the problem of future accumulations of unspent balances. The FY2002 cohort of grantees were the first to experience an expiration of funds; $13 million of FY2002 grant funds expired at the end of FY2008 before they could be used by grantees. FY2003 grantees had about $10 million expire in FY2009 and FY2004 grantees had less than $1 million expire in FY2010.

At the end of FY2010, unspent balances in the HOPE VI fund had been reduced from their peak of $3.3 billion in FY2003 to under $700 million. As illustrated in Figure 2, just about one-third of that amount (33%) is funding that will not expire. The remaining 67% of those funds will expire if not spent within six years of their award.

Over time, the remaining balance of unspent, no-year funds (awarded pre-FY2002) has been declining. As shown in Figure 2, of the $4.9 billion in no-year funding awarded to grantees prior to FY2002, just under $255 million remained at the end of FY2010. That balance has been reduced significantly in recent years; at the beginning of FY2002, the unspent balance of no-year funds was over $3 billion. Outlays among the pre-FY2002 grantees have been relatively constant in recent years, with pre-2002 grantees spending between 20%-30% of their remaining funding each year for the past five years. HUD has taken a number of steps to encourage these earlier grantees to spend their funds, including hiring grant expediters to provide technical assistance to grantees. Also, as noted earlier, HUD has also used poor performance on a HOPE VI grant as a factor in deciding to place a PHA in receivership.

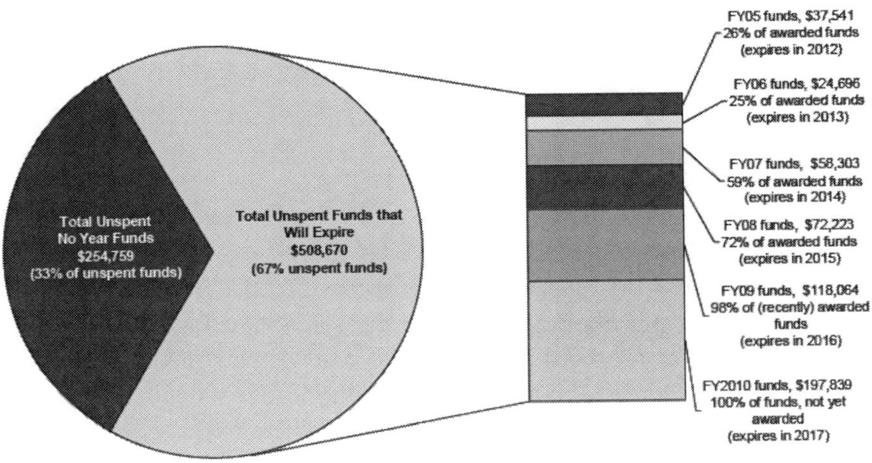

Source: Chart prepared by CRS using data from the Department of Treasury Combined Statement of Receipts, Outlays, and Balances, FY2010.

Figure 2. Composition of Unspent Balances in the Hope VI Program at the End of FY2009 (in thousands of dollars).

Cost-Effectiveness

Over the history of federal housing programs, priorities have shifted from providing publicly constructed and owned housing for low-income families to providing subsidies, either to the private market to build low-cost, private housing, or to residents for use in the private market. One of the main reasons for this shift was the finding that it was more expensive to build and maintain publicly owned housing than it was to provide subsidies to the private market.[22] As a result, the government has not funded the development of new public housing units for many years. Grantees can use HOPE VI funds, in conjunction with other public and private funds, to build replacement units of public housing. Given what is known about the past cost-effectiveness of the construction of public housing, questions can be raised as to whether this is an effective use of limited government dollars. HUD testified before Congress in

2003 that it is not an efficient method. According to the Assistant Secretary for Public and Indian Housing, the division that oversees the HOPE VI program:

> Moreover, it is evident to us that HOPE VI is not an efficient method for meeting the current and future capital needs of the public housing program. The average cost of building a unit under HOPE VI is $120,000, more than 33% greater than the average cost of building a similar unit using the HOME block grant program.[23] Given overall budget constraints, it just doesn't make sense for us to continue funding for this program at the expense of more cost effective programs to serve the same ends.[24]

Taking a different look at the costs of HOPE VI, researchers at the Urban Institute attempted to undertake a cost-benefit analysis of HOPE VI redevelopment compared to maintaining the status quo in distressed public housing. Their study contrasted the up-front costs of undertaking a HOPE VI development (including HOPE VI and other government funding, but excluding equity generated by LIHTCs) to the savings to the government that could result from undertaking the redevelopment. They estimate savings from reduced housing subsidy needs (since new buildings require lower subsidies and are likely to be more energy efficient), improved family well-being (lower welfare, unemployment insurance, Medicaid, and criminal justice system costs), and improved neighborhoods (increased property tax revenue). The Urban Institute study estimates that a prototypical distressed public housing project, undergoing a HOPE VI mixed income redevelopment, could save the government more than $20 million over 20 years.[25]

One-for-One Replacement

The loss of the nation's stock of publicly assisted housing, affordable to low-income families, has been a concern for a number of years. The congressionally mandated, bipartisan Millennial Housing Commission found "a critical shortage of affordable apartments for extremely low-income households."[26] As noted earlier, most HOPE VI developments do not replace every unit of public housing demolished, and most include a number of market rate units that are too expensive for public housing residents to afford. As of March 2006, HOPE VI revitalization grantees planned to demolish 88,469 units of public housing, rehabilitate 10,993 units of existing public housing, and build 92,644 units of new housing—only about half of which would be public housing units, a net loss of 41,000 public housing units. As of March 2006, 88% of the units planned for demolition had been demolished, and 54% of the public housing units slated for construction had been built, an interim net loss of over 50,000 units.

Low-income housing advocates have expressed concern that HOPE VI is eroding the nation's stock of affordable housing, and many have argued that HUD should reinstate the one-for-one replacement requirement. They argue that, in many communities, there is simply a shortage of lower-cost housing and that the federal government has some responsibility to help increase, or at least maintain, the supply.

The requirement that each unit of public housing destroyed be replaced with a new unit of public housing, called "one-for-one replacement," was suspended in 1994 and fully repealed in 1996. Much of the impetus behind the suspension of the requirement was the argument put forward by PHAs that they were unable to deal with troubled public housing because the one-for-one replacement requirement, coupled with site standards, deconcentration requirements, limited funding, and other rules, made the demolition and revitalization process unworkable. At Congress's request, GAO investigated these issues and reported that PHAs were concerned that one-for-one replacement was resulting in developments becoming decrepit.[27] In addition to development concerns, critics of one-for-one replacement argued that it promoted concentrations of poverty, did not appeal to investors, and that the low rents paid by public housing residents would not allow projects to remain financially viable.

PHA groups have contended that reinstating traditional one-for-one replacement will again hamper their ability to undertake housing rehabilitation. Further, there are questions about how one-for-one replacement could affect efforts to deconcentrate poverty. Some compromise strategies, such as requiring some minimum threshold of hard unit replacement, or greater replacement with project-based subsidies, have been considered.

RECENT DEVELOPMENTS

Funding

The Bush Administration requested no new funding for the HOPE VI program in each of his FY2004-FY2008 budget requests to Congress. Citing the slow expenditure of funds, concerns about cost-effectiveness, and that the program had effectively reached its goal of demolishing 100,000 units of distressed public housing, the former Administration stated it was time to rethink whether HOPE VI is still necessary or effective. The Bush Administration argued that even without new funding, the program would not end any time soon because so many projects are still in the pipeline, but that by not funding the program, HUD would have time to throughly evaluate the program and consider alternatives.

Each year, Congress rejected the Bush Administration's request to eliminate funding for the program, but it contined funding at a level significantly less than the amout provided prior to FY2004. (See Table 1 for historical appropriations levels.)

President Obama's first budget in FY2010 requested no new funding for HOPE VI, and instead, requested $250 million for a new Choice Neighborhoods Initiative (discussed later in this report). The final FY2010 funding law, P.L. 111-117, included $200 million for HOPE VI, but of that amount, $65 million was set aside to fund a demonstration of the Choice Neighborhoods Initiative. President Obama's FY2011 budget also requested funding for Choice Neighborhoods, but not for HOPE VI.

HOPE VI Reauthorization

The HOPE VI program was originally authorized through the end of FY2002. The 108th Congress initially extended the program through the end of FY2004 (P.L. 108-7) but later extended the HOPE VI program through the end of FY2006, as a part of a larger bill designed to make changes to a number of housing programs, including HOPE VI. The American Dream Downpayment Act (P.L. 108-186) amended the program to change the selection criteria, broaden the definition of severe distress, require GAO to conduct a study, and add a new category of grant (Main Street Revitalization grants). Several bills to reauthorize the HOPE VI program were introduced in the 109th Congress, although none were enacted. Several reauthorization bills were also considered in the 110th, and one version (H.R. 3524) passed the House. No reauthorization legislation was introduced in the 111th Congress. The program's authorization has been maintained through extensions included in the annual appropriations bills. It is unclear if reauthorization legislation will be considered in the 112th Congress.

Choice Neighborhoods

The Choice Neighborhoods Initiative (CNI) was originally proposed by the Obama Administration as a replacement for the HOPE VI program. The initiative is designed to "transform neighborhoods of poverty into viable mixed income neighborhoods with access to economic opportunity by revitalizing severely distressed public housing and assisted housing and investing and leveraging investment in well-functioning services, effective schools and education programs, public assets, public transportation and improved access to jobs."[28] As described by the Administration, CNI is similar to HOPE VI in that it is a competitive grant program aimed at improving distressed communities. However, it is broader in scope than HOPE VI in that it targets distressed neighborhoods with HUD-assisted housing,[29] not just distressed public housing communities. Key differences between Choice Neighborhoods and HOPE VI, as outlined by the Administration, include the following:

- Eligible Choice Neighborhood grantees may include local governments, nonprofit entities, and for-profit entities partnered with local governments, in addition to PHAs. PHAs are the only eligible grantees in the HOPE VI program.
- While Choice Neighborhood grant funding is to be primarily focused on the transformation of distressed housing, the funding could also be used, on a limited basis, for improvements to the surrounding community. HOPE VI funding can only be used for public housing demolition and development and related supportive services (including relocation).
- Choice Neighborhood grants are targeted to distressed neighborhoods with assisted housing and severely distressed public housing developments. HOPE VI grants are limited to severely distressed public housing developments.

While the Choice Neighborhoods initiative has received some support for its concept of broadening the focus beyond public housing, it has also been met with concerns. Those concerns include whether the program will have the same displacement and loss of affordable housing stock effects as HOPE VI, and whether in a limited funding environment CNI, with its broader pool of eligible applicants, will lead to more entities competing for a limited pot of funds, resulting in less funding available for public housing.

Legislation to authorize the Choice Neighborhoods Initiative was approved by the House Financial Services Committee in the 111th Congress, but was not enacted before the end of the session (H.R. 5814). A Choice Neighborhoods demonstration was funded in FY2010 at $65 million. To date, the FY2010 grants have not been awarded.

End Notes

[1] See William Julius Wilson, *The Truly Disadvantaged: The Inner City, the Underclass and Public Policy* (Chicago: University of Chicago Press, 1987).

[2] For more information on Section 8, see CRS Report RL32284, *An Overview of the Section 8 Housing Programs: Housing Choice Vouchers and Project-Based Rental Assistance*, by Maggie McCarty.

[3] See 42 U.S.C. § 1437v(a).

[4] This list summarizes the definition given in 42 U.S.C. § 1437v(j)(2); the final criteria was not included in QHWRA but was added by P.L. 108-186.

[5] Authorizaton for the program is currently being extended by the FY2011 continuing resolution (P.L. 111-322).

[7] Early in the HOPE VI program, revitalization grants were called implementation grants.

[8] The term "disposition" means the sale or transfer of public housing by the PHA.

[9] The priority groups are, in order of priority, (1) approved for a 202 conversion, (2) applied for a 202 conversion, (3) approved for a Section 18 demolition, or (4) approved for a HOPE VI revitalization grant. Section 202 Mandatory Conversion is the conversion of public housing developments to Section 8. If it costs less to give the residents a Section 8 voucher, rather than maintain the low rent public housing building, the building is shut down and the residents are given Section 8 vouchers. The demolition and disposition of public housing is authorized under Section 18 of the Housing Act of 1937 (the act), as amended. PHAs can apply to demolish public housing, even outside of the HOPE VI program.

[10] U.S. General Accounting Office, *Hope VI Leveraging Has Increased, but HUD Has Not Met Annual Reporting Requirement,* GAO-03-91, November 2002, available at http://www.gao.gov/new.items/d0391.pdf.

[11] According to HUD program summary data, revitalization grantees have demolished 89,892 units of public housing; demolition-only grantees planned to demolish 57,593 units of public housing. Despite the fact that some units may be double-listed, so these figures are not additive, the total demolished likely exceeds 100,000.

[12] Sean Zielenbach, *The Economic Impact of HOPE VI on Neighborhoods* (Washington, DC: Housing Research Foundation, 2002), available at http://www.housingresearch.org/hrf/hrfhome.nsf/e9c24279c3bd4d1085256a0300779c07/dc611c350fe86e7085256cd800698e98/$FILE/ATTSO6UM/ ImpactAnalysisFinal.pdf.

[13] U.S. Government Accountability Office, *HOPE VI Resident Issues and Changes in Neighborhoods Surrounding Grant Sites*, GAO-04-109, November 2003.

[14] For example, see Joanne Huist Smith, "Daytonview Gets Update; Area Has New Look, Feel, Soon to Have New Residents," *Dayton Daily News,* December 25, 2003, p. Z7-1;Vicki Cheng, "Hope in Durham," *The Raleigh News & Observer,* December 8, 2003, p. B1; and

David Austin, "Optimism Marks New Columbia Groundbreaking," *The Oregonian,* December 2, 2003, p. C01.

[15] According to HUD's FY2011 Congressional Budget Justifications, p. M-2.

[16] U.S. Government Accountability Office, *Public Housing: HOPE VI Resident Issues and Changes in Neighborhoods Surrounding Grant Sites* ,GAO-04-109 November 21, 2003.

[17] Jennifer Comey, *HOPE VI'd and On the Move*, Urban Institute, June 2007.

[18] Mary K. Cunningham, Susan J. Popkin, Martha R. Burt, *Public Housing Transformation and the "Hard to House"*, June 2005.

[19] See testimony of George Moses, representing the National Low Income Housing Coalition, and Dr. Susan Popkin from the Urban Institute, before the House Financial Services Subcommittee on Housing and Community Opportunity, June 21, 2007, available at http://www.house.gov/apps/list/hearing/financialsvcs_dem/ht0621072.shtml.

[20] The 1996 grantees are known to have had problems in undertaking their HOPE VI redevelopments. Their problems are especially visible in expenditure data displayed in Figure 2 later in this report. A GAO assessment of 1996 grantees cited several additional factors that have led to delays in HOPE VI projects: PHAs often lack staff with expertise in development and finance, which hinders their ability to undertake complicated mixed-finance deals without acquiring additional staff or consultants; certain types of development, including on-site construction and new construction, are more difficult than others, which may not have been accounted for in original plans; a lack of community and resident support can hinder HOPE VI development plans, and may lead to lengthy litigation; and the HUD approval process can move slowly, perhaps because of staffing limitations.

[21] U.S. General Accounting Office, *HUD's Oversight of HOPE VI Sites Need to Be More Consistent*, GAO-03-555, May 2003, available at http://www.gao.gov/new.items/d03555.pdf.

[22] Mark Shroder and Arthur Reiger, "Vouchers versus Production Revisited," *Journal of Housing Research,* vol. 11, no. 1 (2000), pp. 91-107.

[23] The HUD HOME program provides formula grants to States and localities that communities use—often in partnership with local nonprofit groups—to fund a wide range of activities that build, buy, and/or rehabilitate affordable housing for rent or homeownership or provide direct rental assistance to low-income people.

[24] Testimony of Assistant Secretary for Public and Indian Housing Michael Liu, in U.S. Congress, House Financial Services Committee, Subcommittee on Housing and Community Opportunity, *Strengthening and Rejuvenating Our Nation's Communities and the HOPE VI Program*, hearings, 108th Cong., 1st sess., April 29, 2003, H. Hrg. 108-23 (Washington: GPO, 2003), at http://financialservices.house.gov/media

[25] Margery Austin Turner, Mark Woolley, G. Thomas Kingsley, Susan J. Popkin, Diane Levy, Elizabeth Cove, *Estimating the Public Costs and Benefits of HOPE VI Investments: Methodological Report*, the Urban Institute, July 16, 2007.

[26] Report of the Bipartisan Millennial Housing Commission, *Meeting Our Nation's Challenges* (Washington: GPO, 2002), p. 17.

[27] U.S. General Accounting Office, Public Housing: Funding and Other Constraints Limit Housing Authorities' Ability to Comply with One-for-One Rule, RCED-95-78, March 3, 1995, available at http://archive.gao.gov/t2pbat1/ 153789.pdf.

[28] HUD, "Choice Neighbhorhoods FY2010 NOFA Pre-Notice," May 20, 2010.

[29] Includes public housing, as well as housing financed with Section 8, Section 236, Section 811 or Section 202 contracts.

In: Public Housing: Background and Issues ISBN: 978-1-61324-778-5
Editor: Sara M. Larsen

Chapter 4

Community Service Requirement for Residents of Public Housing*

Maggie McCarty

Summary

The Quality Housing and Work Responsibility Act of 1998 (P.L. 105-276) included provisions designed to promote employment and self-sufficiency among residents of assisted housing, including a mandatory work or community service requirement for residents of public housing. Non-elderly, non-disabled, non-working residents of public housing are required to participate in eight hours per month of either community service or economic self-sufficiency activities in order to maintain their eligibility for public housing. This provision was briefly implemented in FY2001; however, an act of Congress suspended enforcement of the provision in FY2002. That suspension ended in 2003 and residents of public housing are once again required to comply with the community service requirement.

Supporters of the provision believe that it is consistent with the goals of welfare reform and that it will promote civic engagement and "giving back" among residents of public housing; detractors argue that it is punitive, unfair, and administratively burdensome. Legislation was introduced in the 107th, 108th, 109th , 110th , and 111th Congresses to repeal the requirement, although no bills were enacted. In the 111th

* This is an edited, reformatted and augmented version of a Congressional Research Service publication, CRS Report for Congress RS21591, from www.crs.gov, dated January 5, 2011.

Congress, a floor amendment was approved during House floor consideration of the FY2010 HUD appropriations bill (H.R. 3288) that would have prohibited PHAs from using the funding provided in the bill to implement the community service requirement. A contradictory provision supporting the existing requirement was adopted during floor consideration of the Senate version of the bill. The final FY2010 HUD funding law included no changes to the requirement.

This fact sheet describes the provision and its history.

LEGISLATIVE HISTORY

In 1997, H.R. 2, the Housing Opportunity and Responsibility Act of 1997, and S. 462, the Public Housing Reform and Responsibility Act of 1997, were introduced in Congress. Both bills sought to reform the Department of Housing and Urban Development's (HUD) low-income housing programs. The two bills would have consolidated the public housing program into a two-part block grant program; denied occupancy to applicants with a history of drug-related activity; and required residents of public housing to meet a community service requirement. Although both measures passed in their respective houses, they never made it to conference.

On July 17, 1998, the Quality Housing and Work Responsibility Act of 1998 (QHWRA),[1] was offered as an amendment to the FY1999 Departments of Veterans Affairs and Housing and Urban Development (VA-HUD) appropriations bill (H.R. 4194). QHWRA contained several provisions from H.R. 2, including the community service and family self-sufficiency requirements.[2] On October 21, 1998, President Clinton signed QHWRA into law as a part of the FY1999 VA-HUD appropriations bill (P.L. 105-276).

HUD did not issue regulations to implement the community service provisions of QHWRA until March 29, 2000.[3] The regulations took effect beginning on October 1, 2000,[4] and were in effect for just over one year. Language added to the FY2002 VA-HUD appropriations bill (P.L. 107- 73),[5] which was enacted in November 2001, prohibited HUD from using any FY2002 funds to enforce the community service and self-sufficiency requirements, except for residents of HOPE VI developments.[6] The suspension of the provision ended when the FY2003 appropriations bill (P.L. 108-7) was signed into law on February 21, 2003. HUD issued new guidance to the local public housing authorities (PHAs) who administer public housing on June 20, 2003, instructing them to reinstate the community service requirement for public housing residents beginning on August 1, 2003.[7] Specifically, PHAs were required to notify tenants of the requirement by July 31, 2003, and assure that all residents were in compliance by October 31, 2003.[8] The implementation of the requirement was retroactive, meaning that tenants who were not in compliance when the provision was implemented in 2000 were required to make up their previous missing hours in order to be considered in compliance.

COMMUNITY SERVICE AND ECONOMIC SELF-SUFFICIENCY REQUIREMENT[9]

The community service and economic self-sufficiency requirement (community service requirements) applies to all adult residents of public housing who are not otherwise exempted. Exempted residents include residents who are 62 years or older; disabled and can certify that they cannot comply with the requirement; caretakers of a person with a disability; engaged in work activities or exempt from work activities under the Temporary Assistance for Needy Families program (TANF)[10] or a state welfare program; and/or members of a family in compliance with TANF or a state welfare program's work requirements. Given the data that are currently collected, it is hard to gauge exactly how many families are impacted by this requirement. HUD has estimated that approximately 100,000-150,000 households (out of the approximately one million households that live in public housing) include members that are not exempted and therefore must comply with this requirement.

The community service provisions require that residents of public housing, unless exempted, participate in eight hours of community service and/or economic self-sufficiency activities per month. HUD requires that at least eight hours be conducted each month, unless special circumstances warrant an adjustment.[11] PHAs have broad discretion in defining what counts as community service or economic self-sufficiency. Allowable activities include volunteer work at a local public or non-profit institution, caring for the children of other residents fulfilling the community service requirements, participation in a job readiness or training program, and attending a two- or four-year college. The PHA must review and verify each member of a household's compliance 30 days prior to the end of the household's lease. If any member of the household fails to comply with the requirement, the entire household is considered out of compliance. The tenant must agree to make up the community-service deficit in the following year in order to renew the household's lease. If the tenant does not come into compliance, the PHA can not renew the household's lease. However, PHAs may not terminate a household's lease for noncompliance before it has expired. Noncompliant tenants may file a grievance to dispute the PHA's decision.

Each PHA must develop a local policy for administering the community service and economic self-sufficiency requirements and include the policy in its annual plan. PHAs may administer community service activities directly, partner with an outside organization or institution, or provide referrals to tenants for volunteer work or self-sufficiency programs. If the PHA does not administer the activities directly, residents must provide PHAs with a signed certification from a third-party that they have completed the community service activities. Public housing tenants required to fulfill the community service requirements cannot supplant otherwise paid employees of the PHA or other community service organizations.

Issues

The community service and economic self-sufficiency requirement for residents of public housing is consistent with the movement towards required work and self-sufficiency activities in the TANF program. Supporters of mandatory work policies often argue that low income families should "earn" the benefits or subsidies they are receiving. They also argue that by compelling families into self-sufficiency activities, such policies can improve the lives of poor families and their children by potentially increasing their incomes. Those who have argued against mandatory work requirements contend that such requirements are paternalistic and do not promote real self-sufficiency, but rather, low-wage work that may not be sustainable.

There are additional arguments that are made specifically for and against the public housing community service requirement. When the provision was originally debated in 1998, those who supported the requirement specifically for public housing residents argued that, if the requirement resulted in increased earnings for residents of public housing, then the amount of rent paid by tenants would go up. If rents paid by tenants increase, then the cost to the federal government for the program could potentially decrease.

Some members of Congress, during floor debate on the provision, argued that it is unfair to apply this requirement only to residents of public housing and not to recipients of Section 8 vouchers or Section 8 project-based rental assistance, since the programs serve similar populations. Additionally, PHA advocacy groups (such as the National Association of Housing and Redevelopment Officials (NAHRO)) have argued that it is administratively burdensome. Although only a small number of tenants may actually be subject to the requirement, PHAs must certify either the participation or exemption status of every resident of public housing. Furthermore, the grievance and/or eviction process for tenants who are found to be noncompliant with the requirement could be costly. Industry groups contend that this requirement is an unreasonable burden for PHAs, who, they argue, are chronically under-funded. Some of these opponents speculate that PHAs will not aggressively implement the provision, rather, they will try to exempt as many families as possible and set a very broad definition of eligible activities in order to avoid costly grievances and evictions and keep administrative burdens low.

There has also been some controversy surrounding HUD's implementation of the community service requirement. The statute states that in order to meet one of the exemption criteria, tenants must be engaged in work activities, as defined in the Social Security Act. The Social Security Act definition of work activities does not include a minimum number of hours a person must perform the listed activities in order to be considered engaged in work activities. HUD's 2003 Notice to PHAs encouraged them to consider a tenant engaged in work activities, and therefore exempt from the requirement, only if they were working at least 30 hours per week. This guidance initially prompted confusion as to whether PHAs were required to set a 30-hour standard. While the guidance states that PHAs are encouraged to set a 30-hour standard, they do not appear to be required to set such a standard.

In March 2008, HUD's Inspector General released an audit of HUD's implementation and enforcement of the requirement.[12] The audit was performed in response to media reports that the requirement was rarely enforced. The audit found that HUD did not have adequate controls to ensure that PHAs properly administered the requirement, and the audit estimated that at least 85,000 households living in public housing are ineligible as a result of non-compliance with the community service requirement. In response to these findings, in November 2009, HUD published additional guidance to PHAs regarding the administration of the requirements.[13] The guidance largely restated existing requirements, although it did provide enhanced guidance on reporting. It also reiterated steps PHAs may take to enforce the requirement, as well as steps HUD may take to sanction PHAs for failing to enforce the requirement.

LEGISLATION

In recent years, members of Congress have introduced bills to repeal the community service requirement, although none have been enacted. In the 107th Congress (H.R. 2493), the 108th Congress (H.R. 1431), the 109th Congress (H.R. 1018), the 110th Congress (H.R. 458), and the 111th Congress (H.R. 5914), Representative Rangel introduced versions of the Public Housing Tenants Respect Act to repeal the community service requirement for public housing residents.

During House floor consideration of the FY2010 HUD appropriations bill (H.R. 3288), Representative Rangel introduced an amendment (H.Amdt. 376) to prevent the use of funds provided in the bill to enforce the community service requirement. It was approved by voice vote. During floor consideration of the Senate version of the bill, Senator Vitter offered a floor amendment in support of the existing community service requirement, which was approved by a vote of 73-25. The final version of the FY2010 HUD appropriations law (P.L. 111-117) did not contain any provisions related to the community service requirement.

End Notes

[1] For more information on the QHWRA, see CRS Report 98-868, Public Housing and Section 8 Reforms: The Quality Housing and Work Responsibility Act of 1998, by Richard Bourdon.

[2] See Section 512(a)(2) of P.L. 105-276.

[3] See Department of Housing and Urban Development, Changes to Admission and Occupancy Requirements in the Public Housing and Section 8 Housing Assistance Programs; Final Rule, 65 Federal Register 16729, March 29, 2000, which codified the rule at 24 C.F.R. §960.600 et. seq.

[4] Earlier versions of this report mistakenly identified the implementation date as October 1, 2001.

[5] See Section 432 of P.L. 107-73.

[6] The HOPE VI program provides competitive grants to public housing authorities that they can use to revitalize distressed public housing.

[7] See HUD Notice PIH 2003-17 (HA).

[8] Earlier versions of this report mistakenly identified the compliance date as October 1, 2003.

[9] Section 12(c) of the United States Housing Act of 1937, as amended (P.L. 93-383)(42 U.S.C. §1437j).

[10] That statute refers to the Social Security Act definition of work activities (42 USC 607(d)): unsubsidized employment; subsidized private sector employment; subsidized public sector employment; work experience (including work associated with the refurbishing of publicly assisted housing) if sufficient private sector employment is not available; on-the-job training; job search and job readiness assistance; community service programs; vocational educational training (not to exceed 12 months with respect to any individual); job skills

training directly related to employment; education directly related to employment, in the case of a recipient who has not received a high school diploma or a certificate of high school equivalency; satisfactory attendance at secondary school or in a course of study leading to a certificate of general equivalence, in the case of a recipient who has not completed secondary school or received such a certificate; and the provision of child care services to an individual who is participating in a community service program.

[11] Department of Housing and Urban Development, Public Housing Occupancy Guidebook, 2003, p. 176, http://www.disasterhousing.gov/offices/pih/programs/ph/rhiip/phguidebooknew.pdf.

[12] HUD Audit Report 2008-KC-0002, HUD Did Not Ensure That Housing Authorities Property Administered the Community Service and Self-Sufficiency Requirements, March 24, 2008.

[13] HUD Notice PIH 09-48 (HA), Administering the Community Service and Self-Sufficiency Requirement (CSSR), November 25, 2009.

In: Public Housing: Background and Issues ISBN: 978-1-61324-778-5
Editor: Sara M. Larsen

Chapter 5

HUD's Oversight of Housing Agencies Should Focus More on Inappropriate Use of Program Funds*

United States Government Accountability Office

Why GAO Did this Study

The Department of Housing and Urban Development (HUD) provided over $6.7 billion in fiscal year 2008 to housing agencies to operate, modernize, and develop about 1.2 million public housing units. It is important that HUD exercise sufficient oversight of housing agencies to help ensure that public housing funds are being used as intended and properly managed. In this report, GAO examines HUD's oversight processes for detecting housing agencies at risk of inappropriate use and mismanagement of public housing funds. GAO analyzed HUD financial data on about 3,300 housing agencies, compared HUD's oversight policies with program and agency objectives, and interviewed agency officials.

---

* This is an edited, reformatted and augmented version of a United States Government Accountability Office publication, Report to Congressional Addressees GAO-09-33, dated June 2009.

What GAO Recommends

To better focus its oversight processes to identify housing agencies at risk of misuse and mismanagement of public housing funds, GAO recommends that HUD (1) regularly summarize and evaluate the results of audits of public housing agencies to identify common problems, monitor emerging issues, and evaluate overall monitoring and oversight processes; and (2) develop mechanisms—such as financial indicators—and use them as part of its ongoing monitoring and review of housing agencies' use of public housing funds.

In agency comments, HUD stated that the report contains useful information and plans to evaluate alternative ways to address our recommendations.

What GAO Found

Key HUD oversight processes could be more focused on identifying potential inappropriate use or mismanagement of public housing funds. HUD primarily relies on single audits to identify such problems, although HUD, its Office of Inspector General (OIG), and the President's Council on Integrity and Efficiency (now known as the Council of the Inspectors General on Integrity and Efficiency) have identified weaknesses with some audits. Further, even when these audits do identify issues, HUD does not systematically summarize audit findings to identify and understand emerging and persistent issues to better monitor housing agencies for inappropriate use and mismanagement of public housing funds. Understanding these problems could be useful for identifying housing agencies that are at greater risk of inappropriately using or mismanaging public housing funds. HUD uses the Public Housing Assessment System (PHAS) to monitor and rate the overall condition and financial health of public housing agencies. However, PHAS is not intended to identify inappropriate uses of public housing funds and is limited in its ability to detect potential mismanagement. HUD also analyzes the financial data of public housing agencies, but its review focuses on the accuracy and completeness of the information used to calculate PHAS scores. GAO analyzed financial data from the housing agencies and found many housing agencies showed indicators that they were at risk of potential inappropriate use and mismanagement of public housing funds—while most received passing PHAS scores. For example, GAO found that from 2002 to 2006, 200 housing agencies had written checks for more than the funds available in their bank accounts (bank overdrafts) on average of $25,000 or more. However, 75 percent of these agencies received passing PHAS scores (see figure below). Such overdrafts raise questions about these agencies' cash management. But HUD does not use these and similar measures to identify housing agencies at greater risk of inappropriately using or mismanaging public housing funds. Without fully leveraging the audit and financial information it collects, the department limits its ability to identify housing agencies that are at greater risk of inappropriately using or mismanaging program funds.

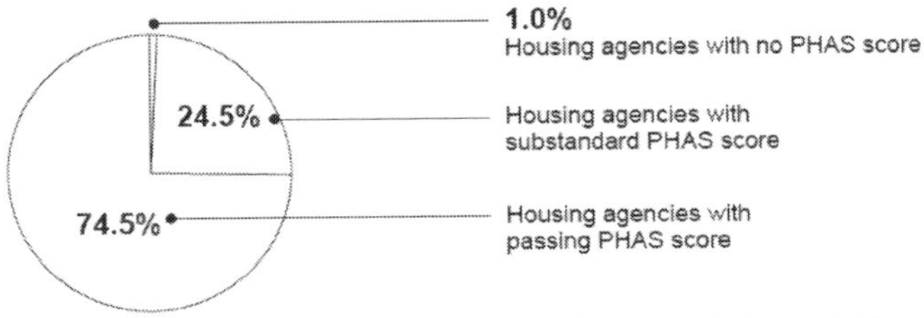

Source: GAO analysis of housing agency financial data schedules and HUD data.

PHAS Scores for the 200 Housing Agencies with Average Bank Overdrafts of $25,000 or More.

ABBREVIATIONS

ARCATS	Audit Resolution and Corrective Actions Tracking System
FASS	Financial Assessment Subsystem
FDS	Financial Data Schedules
HUD	Department of Housing and Urban Development
MAPS	Monitoring and Planning System
MASS	Management Assessment Subsystem
MDHA	Miami-Dade Housing Authority
OIG	Office of Inspector General
OMB	Office of Management and Budget
PASS	Physical Assessment Subsystem
PCIE	President's Council on Integrity and Efficiency
PHAS	Public Housing Assessment System
REAC	Real Estate Assessment Center

June 11, 2009
The Honorable Christopher J. Dodd
Chairman
Committee on Banking, Housing, and Urban Affairs
United States Senate

The Honorable Robert Menendez
Chairman
Subcommittee on Housing, Transportation,
and Community Development
Committee on Banking, Housing and Urban Affairs
United States Senate

In fiscal year 2008, the Department of Housing and Urban Development (HUD) provided approximately $6.7 billion to about 3,300 public housing agencies to subsidize the costs of operating, modernizing, and developing about 1.2 million units through the public housing program. HUD oversees these agencies in cities and communities nationwide to ensure compliance with extensive program requirements. Over the years, we and HUD's Office of Inspector General (OIG) have identified weaknesses in HUD's monitoring of housing agencies' compliance with program requirements and in the agencies' accounting practices as well as instances of misspent public housing funds. A number of recommendations have been made addressing these shortcomings. It is important that HUD exercise adequate oversight of housing agencies' use of public housing funds, and as a result, we undertook a review of HUD's oversight processes under the Acting Comptroller General's authority to conduct evaluations on his own initiative. This report examines the oversight processes HUD employs to identify housing agencies that are at risk of inappropriately using and mismanaging public housing funds.

To evaluate HUD's oversight processes, we compared HUD's oversight policies with its programmatic and agencywide oversight goals. We analyzed housing agency audits and available HUD financial data on its portfolio of housing agencies. We also interviewed HUD headquarters and field office officials. Finally, we met with officials from four field offices and visited nine housing agencies in California, Florida, Maryland, and Washington, D.C. In selecting these sites, we considered various factors, including recent allegations of mismanagement of public housing funds, the activity and size of public housing programs in these locations, and proximity to GAO locations.

We conducted this performance audit from January 2007 through March 2009 in Alameda, Monterey, Richmond, and San Francisco, California; Miami and Fort Lauderdale, Florida; Baltimore and Prince George's County, Maryland; and Washington, D.C. in accordance with generally accepted government auditing standards. Those standards require that we plan and perform the audit to obtain sufficient, appropriate evidence to provide a reasonable basis for our findings and conclusions based on our audit objectives. We believe that the evidence obtained provides a reasonable basis for our findings and conclusions based on the audit objectives. Appendix I provides further details of our objective, scope, and methodology.

RESULTS IN BRIEF

Key HUD oversight processes could be more focused to enable HUD to identify housing agencies that may be at greater risk of inappropriately using or mismanaging public housing funds. The primary process that HUD uses to identify inappropriate use and mismanagement of public housing funds is housing agencies' single audits.[1] Although many single audits have reported problems at individual housing agencies, HUD has found problems with the quality of individual housing agencies' single audits that can limit their reliability. In addition, the President's Council on Integrity and Efficiency (PCIE) issued a report on its National Single Audit Sampling Project in June 2007 that presented compelling evidence that a serious problem with single audit quality continues to exist.[2] Also, annual single audits may not assess compliance with some public housing program requirements administered by these housing agencies, resulting in coverage gaps that may limit the ability of these audits to consistently identify misuse and mismanagement of funds in a timely manner. Despite these limitations, the department continues to primarily rely on single audits to identify potential inappropriate use and mismanagement of public housing funds and is focusing on efforts to improve their quality. Further, even when single and OIG audits report problems, HUD does not maximize the audits' utility by systematically summarizing and analyzing audits that report commonly occurring problems of misuse and mismanagement. Understanding these problems could be useful for evaluating and monitoring HUD's overall monitoring and oversight processes and identifying housing agencies that are at greater risk of inappropriately using or mismanaging public housing funds. For example, the department could use this understanding to develop indicators of potential problems and use these to monitor housing agencies. The department currently uses a system for monitoring and rating the performance of housing agencies—known as the Public Housing Assessment System (PHAS). However, PHAS is limited in its ability to identify housing agencies that may be at greater risk of inappropriate use or mismanagement of funds because it was not designed to detect inappropriate use, and in some cases has not detected housing agencies showing signs of housing fund mismanagement. Further, HUD has stated that its analysis of housing agency financial data is primarily intended to ensure the accuracy of the information that is used to calculate the housing agencies' PHAS scores and not to identify at-risk housing agencies. Our analysis of housing agency financial data illustrates how such data could be leveraged to identify housing agencies at greater risk of inappropriate use or mismanagement of public housing funds that neither PHAS nor the department's current approach to analyzing financial data would detect. For example, our analysis of PHAS and financial data from 2002 through 2006 found that 200 housing agencies had written checks that exceeded the funds available in their bank accounts (bank overdrafts) by $25,000 or more—indicating a potential that these housing agencies could have serious cash and financial management problems and could be prone to increased risk of fraudulent use of funds. However, 75 percent of these agencies received passing PHAS scores. Although HUD has focused its efforts on the challenges of improving the quality of single audits, the department has not taken steps to develop mechanisms to mitigate the limitations of its oversight processes. Without fully leveraging the audit and financial information it collects, the department limits its ability to identify housing agencies that are at greater risk of inappropriately using or mismanaging program funds.

In order to strengthen its oversight of housing agencies administering the public housing program and better leverage information that it already collects, we are recommending that the Secretary of the Department of Housing and Urban Development regularly summarize and systematically evaluate the results of OIG and single audits of public housing agencies to allow program managers to identify and understand problems of potential inappropriate use and mismanagement of public housing funds, identify emerging issues, and evaluate overall monitoring and oversight processes. This report also recommends that the Secretary develop mechanisms— such as financial indicators—to identify housing agencies that are at greater risk of inappropriately using or mismanaging public housing funds.

In written comments on a draft of this report, HUD stated that the report contains useful information but that it did not believe our recommendations would achieve the objectives of strengthening oversight of housing agencies that administer the public housing program and of better leveraging information that it already collects. Although it provided no specific explanation for why it thought our recommendations would not achieve these objectives, HUD stated that more analysis of its existing oversight mechanisms and information collected from housing agencies should be performed in order to evaluate and develop possible alternatives. We welcome HUD's efforts to reconsider the mechanisms and data it uses to oversee housing agencies, but disagree with its statement that our recommendations do not help achieve these objectives. We believe the recommended actions present a reasonable first step in leveraging information it already collects and permit HUD to better focus its limited resources.

BACKGROUND

Under the U.S. Housing Act of 1937, as amended, Congress created the public housing program to provide decent and safe rental housing for eligible low-income families, the elderly, and persons with disabilities.[3] HUD provides subsidies for operating and maintaining public housing units through the Operating Fund.[4] HUD also provides funds to modernize and develop public housing units through the Capital Fund.[5] Public housing agencies administer these formula grant programs on HUD's behalf. In using these funds, the agencies are responsible for ensuring that the housing is affordable to eligible low-income households. In 1992, Congress established the Urban Revitalization Demonstration Program, commonly known as HOPE VI, which provides grants to housing agencies to rehabilitate or rebuild severely distressed public housing.[6]

The Single Audit Act, as amended, requires state and local governments and nonprofit organizations that expend $500,000 or more in federal awards in a fiscal year to have either a single audit or a program-specific audit.[7] Under a single audit, the auditor must report its opinion on the presentation of the entity's financial statements and schedule of federal expenditures, and on compliance with applicable laws, regulations, and provisions of contracts or grant agreements that could have a direct and material effect on the financial statements and, when applicable, on any major program of the audited entity.[8] The auditor must also report the results of its review and testing of internal control related to the financial statements and major programs as well as a schedule of any audit findings and questioned costs. Public housing agencies subject to the act must submit audit reports to HUD and to the Federal Audit Clearinghouse.[9] Single audit is a key assurance process used by HUD in its oversight of public housing agencies. Single auditors are required by the act to identify and test programs for compliance with specific program requirements and report identified findings (or the lack thereof), which can include those of inappropriate use and mismanagement of funds. HUD's Real Estate Assessment Center (REAC), which is responsible for reviewing housing agencies' financial data, began tracking the status of single audit findings in 2007 using the Monitoring and Planning System (MAPS) Audit Tracking Module. Through this tracking system, HUD monitors the resolution of audit findings. HUD maintains an additional system, the Audit Resolution and Corrective Action Tracking System (ARCATS), to monitor the status of management and financial findings issued by our or OIG's recommendations.

HUD's PHAS is another key oversight process. While single audits may identify specific instances of inappropriate use or mismanagement of public housing funds, PHAS was developed to evaluate the overall condition of housing agencies and measure performance in major operational areas of the public housing program. These include financial condition, management operations, and physical condition of the housing agencies' public housing programs as well as resident satisfaction with the programs (see fig. 1).[10]

The Financial Assessment Subsystem (FASS) component score is based on six financial data analyses that HUD has determined to be key in evaluating housing agencies' financial condition. These include the following:

- the current ratio, which measures the housing agency's ability to cover its short-term obligations;
- the months expendable funds balance ratio, which measures the housing agency's reserves for unexpected expenses;
- the tenant receivables outstanding, which measures how well the housing agency manages rent collections;
- the occupancy loss, which measures how well the housing agency maximizes its revenue by renting out vacant units;
- the expense management, which measures whether the housing agency has adequate cost controls to manage expenses; and
- the net income, which measures whether the housing agency is spending more than it makes.

	Financial Assessment Subsystem (FASS) 30 points	**Management Assessment Subsystem (MASS) 30 points**	**Physical Assessment Subsystem (PASS) 30 points**	**Resident Assessment Subsystem (RASS) 10 points**
PHAS components	Measures the financial condition of the housing agency to ensure that it has sufficient financial resources to provide public housing and is managing those resources effectively	Measures a housing agency's management operations capabilities by assessing certain key responsibilities, including site security, work orders, and other aspects of management operations	Measures the physical condition of each of the housing agency's properties to determine if they are decent, safe, sanitary, and in good repair	Measures the level of resident satisfaction with the living conditions of housing provided by the agency

Source: 24 C.F.R. pt 902, Public Housing Assessment System.

Figure 1. Public Housing Assessment System Scoring Subsystem Components.

Housing agencies with scores of less than 60 percent in either the overall PHAS score (less than 60 points out of a total 100 points) or in any one of the major subcomponents, including the FASS (less than 18 points out of 30 points), are designated as substandard performers, also known as troubled.[11] For example, points may be deducted from housing agencies' FASS scores if the six financial analyses indicate that housing agencies are experiencing overall financial difficulties that may threaten the stability of the housing agency. According to HUD officials, although housing agencies' financial data are usually audited, REAC analysts also review financial data to ensure the accuracy of information that is used to calculate the FASS scores. For example, REAC analysts examine specific line items in the financial data, investigate changes or discrepancies in amounts reported, and review auditors' notes.

HUD field offices establish mechanisms to identify and correct deficiencies if a housing agency is designated as a troubled performer in either the PHAS overall score or the FASS subcomponent. Such mechanisms may include the development of an improvement plan or a memorandum of agreement. If technical assistance and sanctions fail to result in significant improvement within a year, the housing agency is referred to the HUD Enforcement Center, which may institute proceedings to place the agency in receivership and remove failed agency management.[12] Receiverships generally result from long-standing, severe, and persistent management problems that have led to the deterioration of the public housing stock.

HUD's Primary Oversight Processes Could Be Better Focused to Detect Housing Agencies at Risk of Inappropriate Uses or Mismanagement of Public Housing Funds

Persistent Problems with Audit Quality and Gaps in What Audits Cover Can Limit HUD's Ability to Detect Misuse or Mismanagement of Public Housing Funds

Single audits, HUD's primary tool for overseeing the use of public housing funds, are intended to, among other things, promote sound financial management by serving as a key accountability mechanism in the oversight and monitoring of recipients' use of federal funds. Single audits provide federal agencies with information on the use of federal funds, internal control deficiencies, and compliance with federal program requirements. The Single Audit Act that mandated the audits does not require the auditors to perform procedures that focus specifically on all federal programs that housing agencies administer. Instead, auditors are to select and closely audit "major" programs administered by the recipient of the funds—typically large or risky programs—for compliance with specific program requirements, including the appropriate use of funds. In addition to single audits, OIG selects various housing agencies to audit as part of its oversight of HUD's public housing program. HUD's strategic goals for its public housing program call for the department to resolve issues identified by these audits and improve its management of internal controls to, among other things, eliminate fraud, waste, and abuse.

However, both HUD's quality assurance office and a recent study conducted by PCIE have identified problems with single audits of housing agencies. OIG also identified problems with single audits after conducting detailed reviews of housing agency operations as part of its oversight process. Both OIG's audits and quality assurance reviews by HUD have, in some cases, resulted in disciplinary action for single auditors. HUD quality control reviews cover housing agency audits as well as audits of other entities that receive HUD financial assistance. According to data from HUD's Quality Assurance Subsystem, 52 of the 247 quality assurance reviews it conducted between 2000 and 2008 resulted in referrals for firms auditing entities receiving HUD funding. According to HUD, many of these included public housing agency audits. Examples of problem public housing agency audits include the following:

- Single audits for the Miami-Dade Housing Authority (MDHA) did not identify significant instances of inappropriate use and mismanagement of funds. In 2006, a media investigation provided extensive coverage of problems with public housing funds at the agency. HUD stated that MDHA's single audits should have alerted the department to these problems, but they did not. Instead, HUD stated that it learned about the allegations of misuse and mismanagement of funds from the *Miami Herald* newspaper in 2006. In response to these allegations, HUD ordered a detailed review and new single audit of the housing agency that found serious and pervasive financial and management problems, including deficiencies in financial management, mismanagement of development funds, and several apparent conflicts of interest. MDHA went into receivership in 2007, with HUD taking possession and control of all of MDHA's activities, including public housing.

- In 2007, OIG found that the Dallas Housing Authority had inaccurate, unreliable, and altered records. Further, OIG noted that the firm conducting the 2006 single audit had failed to meet professional auditing standards. State authorities took disciplinary action against the auditing firm in 2007. According to HUD, the Dallas Housing Authority engaged this firm after it had removed an earlier auditing firm that had identified problems with the housing agencies' financial management.
- Also in June 2007, PCIE issued its Report on National Single Audit Sampling Project, which concluded that there were problems with audit quality that needed to be addressed and made recommendations.[13] Specifically, PCIE reviewed a nationwide sample of 208 out of more than 38,000 single audits performed on various grant recipients that were submitted for the period between April 1, 2003, and March 31, 2004. According to the HUD OIG, the PCIE sample included single audits of 11 housing agencies, of which 6 were determined to be unacceptable, 1 was found to have limited reliability, and 4 were determined to be acceptable, but with deficiencies.

In a 2007 GAO testimony at a congressional hearing on the PCIE study, we noted that problems with the quality of single audits were unacceptable and that we were concerned that audits were not being conducted in accordance with professional standards and requirements.[14] We also noted that such audits could mislead users of audit reports, causing them to incorrectly conclude that agencies were in compliance with program requirements or did not have weaknesses in internal controls when in fact such problems might exist but had gone undetected. However, we also noted continued support for single audits as a key oversight mechanism over federal awards.

Compounding the problems with the quality of audits is the fact that many housing agencies' public housing programs may not have to undergo the detailed major program compliance testing that could potentially uncover inappropriate use and mismanagement of public housing funds. Only entities expending $500,000 or more in federal funding annually are required to receive single audits that assess compliance with specific program requirements and associated internal controls that have a direct and material effect on each major program. Furthermore, even when housing agencies receive single audits, not all public housing programs will be designated as major programs by independent public accountants conducting the single audit. For example, although about 76 percent of operating fund dollars were designated by the housing agencies' independent auditors as major in 2006, less than a third of the housing agencies submitting approved financial data to HUD for that year underwent a single audit and had their operating funds audited as major programs. Without compensating monitoring tools, gaps in coverage at many housing agencies in any one year could allow emerging problems to go undetected and unreported by single audits in a timely manner.

HUD has attempted to improve the quality of these audits but has faced significant challenges. As noted above, HUD performs quality assurance reviews of the independent public auditors who perform the audits. In some cases, these quality assurance reviews have led to investigations and actions against substandard auditors. HUD officials said that the agency could pursue debarment or suspension of poorly performing auditors but noted that such remedies were costly and time-consuming. Further, efforts to improve audit quality will not address gaps in coverage that leave some housing agencies and programs unaudited for more than a year. In light of these limitations, fully leveraging other useful information becomes key to ensuring more consistent monitoring of public housing funds.

HUD Does Not Systematically Summarize the Results of Audits to Understand Problems and Address Vulnerabilities in Its Oversight Processes

Although the quality and coverage of single audits can be problematic, the single audit continues to be an important oversight mechanism. Yet, HUD has not fully leveraged how it uses the results of audits to fully understand emerging or persistent problems at housing agencies. Understanding commonly occurring audit findings could be useful for identifying housing agencies that are at greater risk of inappropriate use or mismanagement of public housing funds and assessing vulnerabilities in HUD's oversight processes. In 2002, we reported that summarizing information about the results of single audits and identifying commonly occurring issues could be valuable in helping management evaluate agency oversight, monitor activities, and identify problem areas.[15] Further, the Domestic Working Group's *Guide to Opportunities for Improving Grant Accountability* states that agencies can summarize the results of internal and external audits for program managers to help identify problems with grantees' financial management and program operations.[16] For example, officials from one federal grant program within the Department of Transportation stated to us that they had taken such an approach to using audit data by summarizing the results of audits to identify recurring issues and direct their oversight policies. These officials stated that their analysis had identified procurement-related problems as a recurring finding area, which resulted in staff conducting grantee workshops and technical assistance on federal procurement requirements.

HUD does track the resolution of individual audit findings for each housing agency. Specifically, HUD uses its ARCATS to track the resolution of the HUD Inspector General's audit findings. In addition, HUD recently developed MAPS to track the resolution of single audit findings. However, on the basis of our discussions with HUD officials, HUD has not used either ARCATS or MAPS to summarize and systematically evaluate the results of audits to understand problems that may commonly occur at multiple housing agencies, identify programwide problems of inappropriate use and mismanagement of public housing funds, detect emerging issues, or address possible vulnerabilities in its oversight processes. HUD's systems contain data that categorize the findings of single audits in a manner that would allow the agency to identify commonly occurring problems across housing agencies. Yet, on the basis of our discussions with HUD, the department has not used these data for this purpose.

We conducted an analysis of a sample of 81 OIG and 56 single audit reports of housing agencies from 2002 through 2007 and categorized the 526 audit findings we identified into major categories of inappropriate use and mismanagement of public housing funds that we developed. Examples of these categories and the number of findings in our sample included: accounting issues, including internal control and documentation findings (150); inappropriate transfer of operating funds to other HUD programs and non-HUD entities, including affiliated organizations that were not used for public housing purposes (98); and other management issues (41). We also noted that for 14 housing agencies where audits identified commonly occurring problems with internal control, documentation, and other management issues, 27 of the findings reported involved management of cash resources. These findings included inadequate separation of duties, fraudulent check writing, and theft of cash.

Such a systematic evaluation of audit results could be useful for program managers, helping them to understand commonly occurring problems, identify and monitor emerging issues, and address limitations in HUD's overall monitoring and oversight processes. Such information could also be useful for HUD field offices, housing agency auditors, and the housing agencies themselves by alerting them to persistent or emerging problems of potential inappropriate use and mismanagement of public housing funds. HUD public housing managers in headquarters and field offices stated that summarized results of audits would aid in helping them carry out their oversight activities. Not effectively using readily available information on the results of audits will continue to hamper these managers' efforts to monitor housing agencies for misuse and mismanagement of funds.

PHAS and HUD's Internal Analyses of Financial Data Could Be Better Focused to Identify Housing Agencies at Risk for Misuse and Mismanagement of Public Housing Funds

PHAS and HUD's internal analyses of data from housing agencies' financial data could be better focused to identify housing agencies that are at greater risk of potential inappropriate uses or mismanagement of public housing funds. As a result, these oversight processes may not alert HUD to potential problems and allow for timely monitoring and additional oversight activities that may be warranted. PHAS primarily assesses data on management operations and the financial health and physical condition of the housing agencies' public housing programs and alerts HUD to potentially troubled agencies. For example, as noted earlier, PHAS was developed to alert HUD to liquidity problems at housing agencies. However, PHAS was never intended to identify individual instances of inappropriate use of public housing funds, and some potential indicators of liquidity problems may not be detected by PHAS. As a result, housing agencies have continued to receive passing PHAS scores even when their financial data may indicate that the housing agency is at greater risk of inappropriately using funds or experiencing serious financial difficulties. HUD has stated that it would primarily rely on single audits to identify such problems.

HUD's policies state that the agency conducts analyses of financial data to help improve public housing agencies' financial health and provide guidance in identifying possible fraud, waste, and abuse. However, HUD told us that it primarily used its analysis of housing agencies' financial statements to ensure the mathematical reasonableness and completeness of the financial data used to calculate housing agencies' PHAS scores. However, we analyzed housing agencies' financial data and found that many of these agencies showed signs that they may be at greater risk of inappropriately using or mismanaging public housing funds, even though the agencies in question received passing PHAS scores.

Potential Inappropriate Use—Improper Advances of Low-Income Public Housing Operating Funds

Our analysis of data from housing agencies' financial statements indicates that many housing agencies receive passing PHAS scores even though an analysis of their financial data indicates that these agencies are at greater risk of inappropriately advancing their public housing program's operating funds to other programs or affiliated entities that may not use the funds for public housing purposes. Both we and OIG found that financial data could be used to identify housing agencies that were potentially at greater risk of inappropriately advancing funds in this manner. Specifically, using financial data, we identified 837 housing agencies that reported balances in their public housing program of over $100,000 as due from other programs—that is, operating funds that were advanced or loaned to other programs or entities and were potentially not used for public housing purposes—between 2002 and 2006. The prior HUD OIG work noted that housing agencies showing balances in excess of $100,000 as due from other programs in their public housing program often inappropriately advanced or loaned public housing program funds to other programs or affiliated entities—such as nonprofit organizations—without these funds being repaid to the public housing program. For example, OIG noted instances where public housing funds were advanced inappropriately and used for private housing development. In response to these OIG audits, HUD reported that it had taken steps to resolve audit recommendations and had made referrals for administrative action to be taken against those housing agencies. HUD further recognized that housing agencies showing large amounts in their due from other funds accounts may warrant greater scrutiny and analyses of transactions.

Our analysis of housing agencies' due from other program accounts shows that from fiscal years 2002 through 2006, about 15 to 17 percent of housing agencies exhibited this indicator of possible inappropriate advances ($100,000 or more as due from other programs). (See fig. 2.)

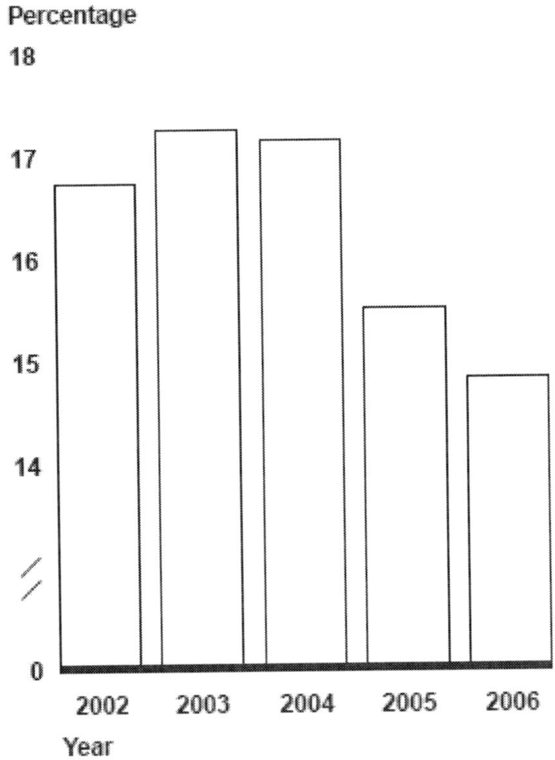

Figure 2. Percentage of Housing Agencies with Potentially Improper Advances of Operating Funds (Balances Due from Other Programs in Excess of $100,000), Fiscal Years 2002-2006.

While these housing agencies' financial data were showing that these agencies were at greater risk of inappropriately advancing operating funds, their PHAS scores may not have provided HUD with any indication of this potential risk. PHAS assesses the overall management operations and the financial and physical condition of the housing agencies' public housing programs, but it was not developed to identify potential inappropriate use of funds, such as inappropriate advances of operating funds. Our analysis found that about 80 percent of the housing agencies that reported balances in excess of $100,000 in the operating fund's due from other program from fiscal years 2002 through 2006 received passing scores in PHAS (see fig. 3). Thus, the PHAS score by itself would not identify or trigger any further oversight of housing agencies that may be at risk of potential improper advancement of funds.

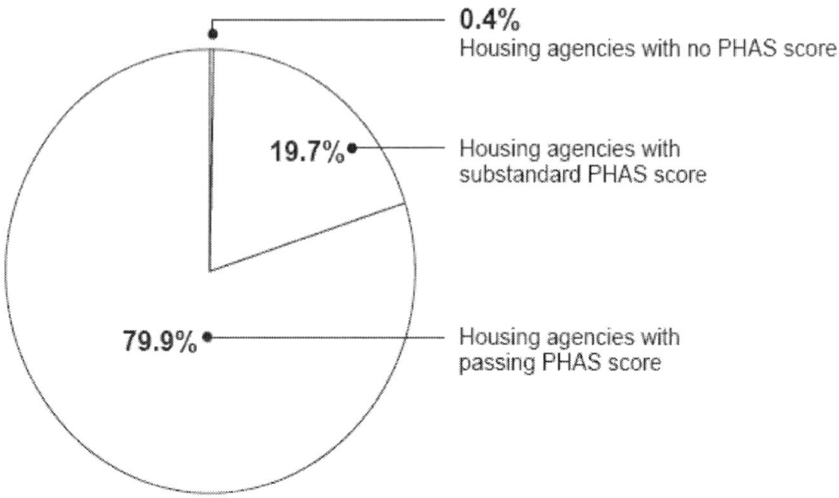

Source: GAO analysis of housing agency financial data schedules and HUD data.
Note: Some housing agencies are not required to submit PHAS scores for various reasons. For example, two housing agencies were not required to submit PHAS scores because they are in the Moving to Work program.

Figure 3. PHAS Scores for Housing Agencies with Potential Improper Operating Fund Advances (Balances Due from Other Programs in Excess of $100,000), Fiscal Years 2002–2006.

HUD officials stated that they would continue to rely on single audits to identify improper advances of this nature despite concerns about the quality of single audits and gaps in the number of housing agencies and programs covered and that they do not conduct specific financial analyses to identify housing agencies at risk of inappropriate advances of their operating funds. However, HUD does perform analyses of financial data to help it identify housing agencies that are at risk of improper advances for a HUD rental housing program—the Housing Choice Voucher program.[17] Specifically, HUD conducts an assessment of housing agencies' financial data to identify housing agencies reporting transfers of voucher program dollars that warrant additional oversight. Analyzing operating fund financial data as it has with the Housing Choice Voucher program illustrates how the department could leverage opportunities to identify and monitor housing agencies at greater risk of inappropriate advances of public housing funds.

Potential Mismanagement of Funds—Poor Cash Management

Our analysis also indicated that some housing agencies showed signs that they are at greater risk of mismanaging public housing funds. For example, we found that some housing agencies reported check overdrafts in their financial data. Our analysis of housing agencies' financial data for fiscal years 2002 through 2006 showed 200 housing agencies reporting average bank overdrafts of $25,000 or more, and 10 housing agencies reporting average bank overdrafts of more than $1 million. The vast majority of housing agencies do not show this indicator of potential funds mismanagement. In fact, over 92 percent of all housing agencies reported no check overdrafts during this period. According to HUD's OIG, writing checks in excess of funds available in a housing agency's bank account is of concern and could indicate serious cash and financial management problems or indicate that the housing agency is prone to potential fraud. MDHA provides an example of how check overdrafts could have been used as an indicator of serious liquidity problems. Specifically, HUD audits noted that MDHA was consistently holding checks in a safe after it had written them and reported the millions of dollars in these checks as bank overdrafts in the housing agency's financial data. HUD officials overseeing the receivership of MDHA stated that the housing agency was taking this action because it did not have the funds available to meet its financial obligations. MDHA's single audits for this period were later determined to be substandard, in part because they did not identify an accounting misclassification of cash that may have masked the agency's liquidity problems.

HUD officials stated that housing agencies' PHAS and FASS scores were used to alert the agency to potential issues with finances and liquidity. However, we found that housing agencies' PHAS and FASS scores did not reflect the large bank overdrafts that we identified. Of the 10 housing agencies reporting bank overdrafts in excess of $1 million, 7 (including MDHA) received passing PHAS scores. Only 1 had a PHAS score indicating that the agency was troubled. Further, MDHA received a passing FASS score for 3 of 5 years included in our analysis. The remaining 2 agencies were exempted from reporting PHAS scores because of their participation under the Moving to Work program.[18] As shown in figure 4, when we looked at the 200 housing agencies reporting an average bank overdraft of $25,000 or more from 2002 through 2006, we found that nearly 75 percent of these housing agencies received passing PHAS and FASS scores.

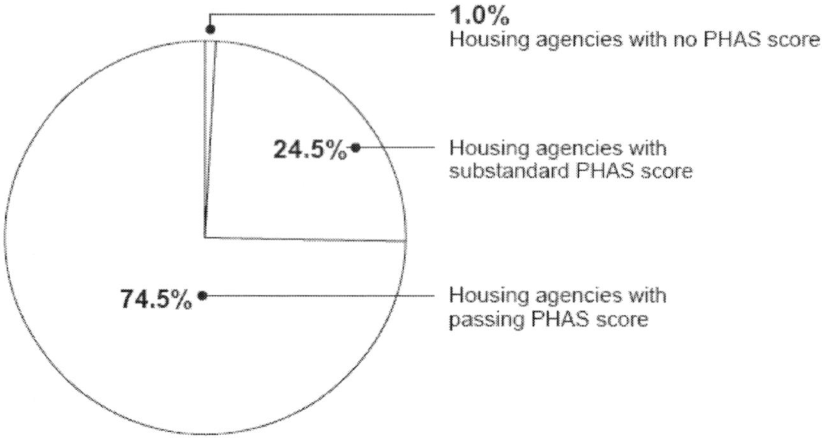

Source: GAO analysis of housing agency financial data schedules and HUD data.

Figure 4. PHAS Scores for Housing Agencies with Potential Funds Mismanagement (Average Bank Overdrafts in Excess of $25,000), Fiscal Years 2002–2006.

HUD officials stated that they were concerned about housing agencies with substantial bank overdrafts but added that overdrafts were not flagged for further monitoring because PHAS and single audits were expected to detect such poor financial management. However, as we have seen, single audits, PHAS, and the department's current approach to analyzing financial data do not always detect or alert HUD to housing agencies at greater risk of potential inappropriate use or mismanagement of public housing funds. This shortcoming underscores the importance of leveraging the financial data HUD collects to focus on housing agencies at risk of these potential problems. For example, HUD could use financial indicators to identify housing agencies that are at greater risk of such problems. HUD could then use the information to alert its field offices, auditors, and the housing agencies themselves to potential problems. Developing such indicators of potential inappropriate use and mismanagement could also be a particularly useful compensating mechanism for monitoring housing agencies that are not subject to single audits and a valuable monitoring tool to mitigate the limitations of PHAS. Not fully leveraging the information it already has limits HUD's ability to identify potential waste and abuse of its resources.

CONCLUSIONS

HUD relies on single audits to identify potential misuse and mismanagement of public housing funds, and many single audits as well as those of OIG have identified such problems. However, concerns about the quality of single audits and gaps in the coverage of these audits have limited HUD's confidence that single audits will consistently identify inappropriate use and mismanagement of public housing funds at every housing agency. Although HUD has faced difficulty in making improvements to the quality of audits and is aware that many housing agencies' public housing programs may not receive annual single audit coverage, it has not adapted the way it uses information it collects to develop mechanisms to mitigate these limitations. Specifically, HUD does not systematically summarize and analyze the types and causes of misuse and mismanagement that single and OIG audits do successfully identify. Understanding the attributes of these commonly occurring problems that single and OIG audits have found could be useful to public housing program managers in identifying emerging issues and evaluating HUD's overall monitoring and oversight processes. Promising practices identified by the Domestic Working *Group's Guide to Opportunities for Improving Grant Accountability* call for such efforts. In fact, our review of over 130 audits conducted between 2002 and 2007 showed almost 100 findings related to inappropriate advancement of public housing operating funds to non-HUD programs or entities. Summarized results could also be useful to HUD's field offices, auditors, and the housing agencies themselves, helping them understand emerging and persistent issues in HUD's national portfolio of housing agencies and carry out their responsibilities in monitoring public housing programs.

HUD currently uses PHAS to monitor housing agencies, but this system has not always identified housing agencies at risk of problems such as cash management issues and was not intended to identify inappropriate use of public housing funds. Although HUD has developed automated checks of housing agencies' financial information to help ensure its completeness and accuracy for PHAS, the department has not used these checks as a mechanism to identify housing agencies at greater risk for potential misuse and mismanagement of public housing funds. HUD itself uses such checks to identify potential inappropriate use of its Housing Choice Voucher Program funds. Fully utilizing data HUD collects—for example, by developing financial indicators to help identify housing agencies at greater risk of inappropriately using or mismanaging public housing funds—would help in developing tools to compensate for the limitations of key oversight processes.

RECOMMENDATIONS FOR EXECUTIVE ACTION

In order to strengthen its oversight of housing agencies administering the public housing program and better leverage information that it already collects, we recommend that the Secretary of the Department of Housing and Urban Development:

- Regularly summarize and systematically evaluate the results of OIG and single audits of public housing agencies to allow program managers to identify and understand problems of potential inappropriate use and mismanagement of public housing funds, identify emerging issues, and evaluate overall monitoring and oversight processes. Summarized results of audits should be disseminated to field offices, housing agencies, and their auditors to help make them aware of emerging or persistent problems and assist them in monitoring and administering HUD's public housing programs.
- Develop mechanisms—such as financial indicators—to identify housing agencies that are at greater risk of inappropriately using or mismanaging public housing funds. Such mechanisms may be developed based on the department's evaluation of commonly occurring and emerging issues identified in OIG and single audits of housing agencies and developed by leveraging financial information that the department currently collects. Once such indicators are developed, the department should use them as part of its ongoing monitoring and review of housing agencies' use of public housing funds.

AGENCY COMMENTS AND OUR EVALUATION

In written comments from the General Deputy Assistant Secretary for Public and Indian Housing (see app. II), HUD stated that the draft report contains useful information, but that the agency did not believe that our recommendations would achieve the objectives of strengthening oversight of housing agencies that administer the public housing program and of better leveraging information that it already collects. Although it provided no specific explanation for why it thought our recommendations would not achieve its objectives, HUD stated that more analysis of its existing oversight mechanisms and information collected from housing agencies should be performed in order to evaluate and develop possible alternatives and indicated that it would involve Public and Indian Housing parties in developing a more creative and comprehensive approach to addressing the issues raised in our report. We welcome efforts by HUD to reconsider the mechanisms and data it uses to oversee housing agencies and to identify opportunities for improving its oversight. However, we disagree with HUD's statement that our recommendations do not help achieve the objectives of strengthening its oversight and better leveraging the audit and financial information it already has. We believe the recommended actions present a reasonable first step in leveraging its existing information and permit HUD to better focus its limited resources. In fact, as noted in the report, the mechanisms that we are recommending for identifying potential problems to identify housing agencies that are at risk of inappropriate use of funds are already being used by another key HUD rental assistance program and by the HUD OIG. Moreover, HUD has in place systems that capture the information needed for such analysis. As HUD reevaluates its oversight mechanisms and seeks the input of its new Assistant Secretary, we believe that thinking about ways of leveraging the information it receives from single audits and financial data will be helpful in identifying emerging issues related to inappropriate use and mismanagement of funds and in providing the oversight necessary to address these issues.

Mathew J. Scirè
Director, Financial Markets
and Community Investment

APPENDIX I: OBJECTIVE, SCOPE, AND METHODOLOGY

This report evaluates the Department of Housing and Urban Development's (HUD) oversight of public housing agencies' use of federal funds to operate, modernize, and develop public housing units through the Operating Fund, Capital Fund, and HOPE VI programs—the three main sources of funding for the public housing program. In 2008, the Operating Fund, Capital Fund, and HOPE VI programs provided approximately $6.7 billion to housing agencies for capital asset management. The objective of this report was to examine the oversight processes HUD uses to understand and detect instances of inappropriate use and mismanagement of public housing funds.

We reviewed applicable federal laws and regulations to describe permissible uses for the public housing funds within the scope of this report—specifically, funds available under the Operating Fund, Capital Fund, and HOPE VI programs. To describe HUD processes to ensure that housing agencies use public housing funds for statutorily allowable uses, we reviewed pertinent federal laws, agency notices, and program guides, and other job aids or documents. We interviewed program officials in the Office of Public and Indian Housing, including administrators from the Offices of the Deputy Secretary for Field Operations and of the Deputy Secretary for Public Housing Investments in Washington, D.C. We obtained information on the Public Housing Assessment System (PHAS) and financial management assessment procedures from officials responsible for this system at HUD's Real Estate Assessment Center (REAC). In addition, we reviewed key documents that describe the annual single audit process as applicable to housing agencies that receive federal funds, such as the Office of Management and Budget's (OMB) Circular A133: *Audits of States, Local Governments, and Non-Profit Organizations* and HUD program documents.

We also interviewed officials from four HUD field offices and obtained additional documentary and testimonial information to summarize the oversight processes. We selected field offices for review. We selected the HUD field office in Miami-Dade because it oversaw the Miami-Dade Housing Authority, which had been the most recent housing agency to go into receivership pursuant to a settlement agreement resolving allegations of financial mismanagement. We also met with officials from three other HUD field offices: Baltimore, San Francisco, and Washington, D.C. Within their portfolios, these field offices all have housing agencies with active Operating Fund, Capital Fund, and HOPE VI programs, with a range of housing agencies of different sizes, and in proximity to cities near GAO offices. Although the results of our discussion with these field offices may not be generalized across all field offices, our discussions provided important context on HUD's implementation of its oversight processes and corroboration of information we collected. We also obtained information on HUD's oversight procedures with staff from selected public housing agencies in each of the HUD field office locations: the Housing Authority of the City of Alameda, Housing Authority of the County of Monterey, Richmond Housing Authority, and San Francisco Housing Authority in California; the Miami-Dade Housing Authority and Housing Authority of the City of Fort Lauderdale in Florida; the District of Columbia Housing Authority; and the Housing Authority of Baltimore City and Prince George's County Housing Authority in Maryland.

To understand commonly occurring reported findings of inappropriate use or mismanagement of public housing funds by housing agencies, we conducted a content analysis of findings in HUD's Office of Inspector General (OIG) audit and single audit reports of housing agencies. Through this analysis we developed a number of categories and subcategories of common findings reported in these audits, including instances of noncompliance and internal control deficiencies. We took steps to ensure that the categories and subcategories we developed were consistently applied across both OIG and single audit reports, which included independent verification that the established categories and subcategories in the OIG reports were applicable to the findings we analyzed in the single audit reports. To select OIG audits for our analysis, we obtained a list of all audit reports with findings related to the three public housing funds (Operating Fund, Capital Fund, and HOPE VI) from 2002 through 2007. This list contained 144 audit reports. We also determine whether these audits met the following additional criteria for inclusion in our content analysis sample: (1) The audit findings were related to inappropriate use of funds and mismanagement issues, and (2) the audits were initiated by OIG or entities other than HUD program officials. We identified 81 OIG audits that met these criteria and constituted our final sample.

Single audit reports for our analysis were selected from audits conducted from audit years 2002 through 2005. This period differs from one for our analysis of OIG audit report because single audit reports are not due to HUD or to the Federal Audit Clearinghouse—the source from which we drew our sample—until 9 months after a housing agency's fiscal year end. As a result, some housing agencies had not yet submitted their 2006 or 2007 single audit reports by the time we performed our analysis. Using HUD financial data on housing agencies, we created a list of 129 single audit reports with findings related to the three public housing funds from audit years 2002 through 2005. We ensured that these single audit and OIG reports related to financial management issues within the scope of our review. Our final sample of 56 reports included 8 reports in 2002, 10 in 2003, 18 in 2004, and 20 in 2005.

To identify potential cases of housing agencies at greater risk of inappropriately using or mismanaging funds across the HUD housing agency portfolio, we reviewed financial information from REAC's financial data schedule (FDS) database for approximately 3,300 housing agencies. We reviewed HUD's *Financial Data Schedule Line Definition and Crosswalk Guide* on the data fields available in this system and analyzed certain data line items. Specifically, we identified those FDS line items that could be used to assess potential areas of inappropriate use and financial mismanagement. In particular, we looked at FDS information on advances of public housing funds as a potential indicator of improper use and on cash management (bank overdrafts) as a potential indicator of financial mismanagement. At the time that we obtained these data from HUD, fiscal year 2006 was the last year for which a full year of financial data schedules was available.

We assessed the reliability of the data by (1) reviewing existing information about the systems and the data, (2) interviewing agency officials knowledgeable about the data, and (3) examining data elements used in our work by conducting electronic edit checks and comparing actual with anticipated values. For the FDS data, we analyzed the most current available data from the system for the years within the scope of our review. We obtained explanations on inconsistencies we found in the data from agency officials. We determined that the data were sufficiently reliable for the purposes of this report.

Analysis of potential inappropriate use of funds: As a potential indicator of inappropriate use, such as improper advances of funds, we analyzed balances of funds due from other program (FDS line item 144) for all housing agencies' operating funds from fiscal years 2002 through 2006. We selected this line item because HUD's OIG has identified housing agencies that have inappropriately advanced public housing operating funds by analyzing FDS for housing agencies that reported balances in excess of $100,000 on line item 144 for the operating fund. OIG found that housing agencies often used the public housing general fund bank account as the payment account for various other activities of the housing agency. When these other activities did not repay the operating fund account, a balance was reported on line 144 of the FDS. When housing agencies did this for activities requiring substantial amounts of cash, the balance in line 144 tended to grow, indicating an inappropriate use of funds. Similarly, we identified housing agencies showing amounts due from other program balances in excess of $100,000 for its operating fund as an indicator of potential inappropriate advances of funds.

Analysis of potential mismanagement of funds: To identify housing agencies that may have fund mismanagement problems, such as poor cash management, we analyzed amounts reported as bank overdrafts in FDS (line item 311). This line item on FDS represents checks written in excess of funds available in bank accounts. In identifying this line item as an indicator of potential fund mismanagement, we interviewed HUD officials to determine if there were sound or legitimate operational reasons for a housing agency writing checks in excess of funds available in a housing agency's bank account. HUD officials could not provide such reasons. Further, OIG agreed that using bank overdrafts as an indicator of potential funds mismanagement was reasonable.

We conducted this performance audit from January 2007 through March 2009 in Alameda, Monterey, Richmond, and San Francisco, California; Miami and Fort Lauderdale, Florida; Baltimore and Prince George's County, Maryland; and Washington, D.C. in accordance with generally accepted government auditing standards. Those standards require that we plan and perform the audit to obtain sufficient, appropriate evidence to provide a reasonable basis for our findings and conclusions based on our audit objectives. We believe that the evidence obtained provides a reasonable basis for our findings and conclusions based on the audit objectives.

APPENDIX II: COMMENTS FROM THE U.S. DEPARTMENT OF HOUSING AND URBAN DEVELOPMENT

U.S. DEPARTMENT OF HOUSING AND URBAN DEVELOPMENT
WASHINGTON, DC 20410-5000

OFFICE OF PUBLIC AND INDIAN HOUSING

MAY 27 2009

Mr. Mathew J. Scire
Director
Financial Markets and Community Investment
U. S. Government Accountability Office
441 G Street, NW
Washington, DC 20548

Dear Mr. Scire:

The Office of Public and Indian Housing has reviewed the draft report on HUD's Oversight of Housing Agencies Should Focus More on Inappropriate Use of Program Funds (GAO-09-33). Enclosed are my written comments concerning your report. As noted in the enclosed comments, I will be discussing your recommendations with the new Assistant Secretary for Public and Indian Housing when she arrives.

Please contact Michael Mangahas at (202) 402-6726, if you have any questions.

Sincerely,

Paula O. Blunt
General Deputy Assistant Secretary
for Public and Indian Housing

Enclosure

www.hud.gov espanol.hud.gov

Public and Indian Housing Comments on
HUD's Oversight of Housing Agencies Should Focus More on Inappropriate Use of Program Funds (GAO-09-33)

Overall PIH Response to GAO Draft Review Report

Your Report contains useful information and provided PIH with recommendations on how to strengthen oversight of housing agencies (PHAs) administering the public housing program and to better leverage information that it already collects. However, PIH does not believe that the recommendations provided will accomplish these objectives.

It is anticipated that the new Assistant Secretary for PIH will be arriving soon. PIH would like the opportunity to brief the new Assistant Secretary on the GAO report and allow her the opportunity to decide how she wants to approach the issues that have been raised.

Recommendations for Executive Action

1. **Regularly summarize and systematically evaluate the results of OIG and single audits of public housing agencies to allow program managers to identify and understand problems of potential inappropriate use and mismanagement of public housing funds, identify emerging issues, and evaluate overall monitoring and oversight processes. Summarized results of audits should be disseminated to field offices, housing agencies, and their auditors to help make them aware of emerging or persistent problems and assist them in monitoring and administering HUD's public housing programs.**

2. **Develop mechanism—such as financial indicators—to identify housing agencies that are at greater risk of inappropriately using or mismanaging public housing funds. Such mechanisms may be developed based on the department's evaluation of commonly occurring and emerging issues identified in OIG and single audits of housing agencies and developed by leveraging financial information that the department currently collects. Once such indicators are developed, the department should use them as part of its ongoing monitoring and review of housing agencies' use of public housing funds.**

PIH response:

PIH believes that more analysis of the existing oversight mechanisms and information collected from PHAs should be done in order to evaluate and develop possible alternatives. We need additional time to involve other PIH parties in developing a more creative and comprehensive approach in resolving these issues.

As previously noted, the draft report will be discussed with the new Assisted Secretary once she reports to HUD.

End Notes

[1] The Single Audit Act of 1984, as amended, Pub. L. No. 98-502, 98 Stat. 2327, *codified at* 31 U.S.C. § 7501- 7507, requires state and local governments and nonprofit organizations that expend $500,000 or more in federal awards in a fiscal year to have either a single audit or a program-specific audit.

[2] PCIE had been established under an Executive Order, but the PCIE is being terminated and replaced with the Council of the Inspectors General on Integrity and Efficiency, as provided by the Inspector General Reform Act of 2008. Pub. L. No. 110-409, 122 Stat. 4302. Currently, PCIE is known as the Council of the Inspectors General on Integrity and Efficiency (CIGIE).

[3] Ch. 896, 50 Stat. 888.

[4] 42 U.S.C. § 1437g(e)(1).

[5] 42 U.S.C. § 1437g(d)(1).

[6] 42 U.S.C. § 1437v.

[7] 31 U.S.C. § 7502(a). See Office of Management and Budget (OMB) Circular A-133. The single audit threshold was raised from $300,000 to $500,000 for fiscal years ending after December 31, 2003. 68 Fed. Reg. 38401 (June 27, 2003). Election of program-specific audits can occur when an auditee expends federal awards under only one federal program (other than for research and development) and when federal laws, regulations, or grant agreements do not require a financial statement audit of the auditee. Under these circumstances, the auditee may elect to have a program-specific audit, which is limited to the auditee's finances, controls, and compliance under the program.

[8] OMB prescribes guidance for determining which programs are major for the audited entity and includes criteria such as the amount of federal awards expended by the entity and other risk factors. OMB also publishes a document called the *Compliance Supplement* that summarizes the laws, regulations, and other program requirements that generally apply to all federal programs and some that apply specifically to public housing and other federal programs. We did not review the adequacy or completeness of the compliance requirements for public housing programs identified by OMB in the *Compliance Supplement.*

[9] The Federal Audit Clearinghouse single audit database was established as a result of the Single Audit Act Amendments of 1996 (Pub. L. No. 104-156, 110 Stat. 1396) and contains summary information on the auditor, the recipient and its federal programs, and the results of audits.

[10] There are special circumstances for which housing agencies may opt out of some PHAS reporting requirements. Standard/high-performing housing agencies that have fewer than 250 units may skip some components of PHAS, except the financial evaluation, every other year. Housing agencies affected by a disaster can obtain a waiver from HUD to exempt them from PHAS reporting. Also, some of the housing agencies designated by HUD as part of the Moving to Work program, a demonstration program authorized by Congress that provides certain housing agencies greater flexibility in financial and program management, may be exempted, depending on their particular arrangements with HUD.

[11] For the purposes of this report, GAO considered a PHAS score to be passing for any housing agency with an overall PHAS composite score that was not less than 60 percent and/or with a FASS score that was not less than 60 percent.

[12] When troubled housing agencies with 1,250 or more units cannot improve their overall PHAS scores to 60 or their subcomponent scores to 18 within 2 years, the Quality Housing and Work Responsibility Act of 1998 (Pub. L. No. 105-276, title V, 112 Stat. 2518) directs HUD to take action against them, including appointing a receiver. 42 U.S.C. § 1437d(j)(3)(B)(III).

[13] See PCIE, *Report on National Single Audit Sampling Project*, June 2007.

[14] GAO, *Single Audit Quality: Actions Needed to Address Persistent Audit Quality Problems*, GAO-08-213T (Washington, D.C.: Oct. 25, 2007).

[15] GAO, *Single Audit: Actions Needed to Ensure That Findings Are Corrected*, GAO-02-705 (Washington, D.C.: June 26, 2002).

[16] The guide provides information for government agencies, identifies areas for potential improvement in grant oversight, and highlights specific examples of promising practices that federal agencies have implemented, although it does not evaluate the effectiveness of the practices. For example, the guide discusses using internal and external audits to identify at-risk grantees and summarizing audit results to support future management decisions. Formed by GAO in 2001, the Domestic Working Group is an intergovernmental group made up of 19 federal, state, and local audit organizations that was tasked by the Comptroller General of the United States with suggesting ways of improving grant accountability.

[17] Housing choice vouchers are administered locally by public housing agencies. Housing agencies receive funds from HUD to administer the voucher program. A family that is issued a housing voucher is responsible for finding a suitable housing unit of the family's choice where the owner agrees to rent under the program. See 42 U.S.C. § 1437f(o).

[18] The Moving to Work program offers housing authorities the opportunity to design and test innovative, locally designed housing and self-sufficiency strategies for low-income families by allowing exemptions from existing public housing and tenant-based Housing Choice Voucher rules and permitting housing agencies to combine operating, capital, and tenant-based assistance funds into a single agencywide funding source, as approved by HUD. Pub. L. No.104-134, 110 Stat. 1321(1996).

INDEX

A

abolition, 10
abuse, 24, 113, 117, 122
access, 25, 43, 44, 91
accountability, 14, 112, 133
accounting, 31, 41, 59, 61, 106, 116, 121
adjustment, 97
administrators, 126
adults, 31, 67
advancement, 119, 123
advocacy, 99
age, 31, 38, 51, 56
agencies, viii, 13, 17, 26, 39, 52, 55, 56, 64, 69, 72, 103, 104, 106, 107, 108, 109, 110, 112, 113, 114, 115, 116, 117, 118, 119, 120, 121, 122, 123, 124, 125, 126, 127, 128, 129, 132, 133
alcohol abuse, 24
American Recovery and Reinvestment Act, 40, 41, 48, 54
American Recovery and Reinvestment Act of 2009, 41, 48, 54
appropriations, 2, 6, 37, 39, 40, 43, 48, 54, 62, 63, 64, 66, 68, 70, 71, 72, 73, 74, 85, 90, 96, 100
Appropriations Act, 26, 50
assessment, 10, 16, 19, 50, 53, 93, 120, 126
assessment procedures, 126
assets, 20, 91
assisted housing, viii, 21, 23, 66, 81, 91, 95
audit, 14, 99, 104, 107, 109, 113, 114, 115, 116, 118, 123, 125, 126, 127, 128, 129, 131, 132, 133
audits, 104, 106, 107, 108, 110, 112, 113, 114, 115, 116, 117, 118, 120, 121, 122, 123, 124, 125, 127, 128, 132, 133
authorities, vii, 1, 3, 4, 10, 12, 47, 55, 66, 67, 96, 100, 114, 133
authority, 10, 12, 17, 44, 47, 48, 79, 106

B

background information, 42
barriers, 24, 67, 83
benefits, 16, 34, 35, 46, 98
bonds, 7, 39
breakdown, 12, 76
Bush Administration, viii, 40, 65, 73, 89, 90
business partners, 28

C

candidates, 43
Capital Fund Financing program (CFFP), 39
capital markets, 44, 83
cash, 48, 68, 105, 108, 116, 121, 123, 128, 129
Census, 30, 53, 82
certificate, 101

certification, 98
challenges, 108, 115
Chicago, 92
children, 1, 3, 22, 26, 31, 33, 34, 35, 36, 46, 50, 53, 68, 71, 84, 97, 98
cities, 28, 70, 75, 82, 106, 127
citizens, 20
City, 13, 92, 127
civil rights, 7, 20
Clinton Administration, 10
coal, 51
color, 6
commercial, 18, 82, 83
common findings, 127
communities, viii, 3, 5, 6, 9, 12, 14, 20, 25, 28, 35, 39, 45, 52, 65, 67, 68, 69, 70, 71, 72, 78, 81, 82, 83, 84, 89, 91, 93, 106
community, viii, 7, 11, 12, 14, 15, 19, 20, 23, 25, 28, 34, 49, 53, 66, 70, 75, 76, 78, 79, 82, 83, 85, 91, 93, 95, 96, 97, 98, 99, 100
community service, viii, 11, 15, 23, 34, 95, 96, 97, 98, 99, 100
competition, 4
competitive grant program, 2, 91
competitive process, 85
compliance, 23, 59, 97, 99, 100, 106, 107, 109, 113, 114, 132
composition, 23, 51
computing, 59
conference, 96
Congress, viii, 1, 6, 7, 8, 9, 10, 11, 19, 28, 37, 39, 41, 42, 43, 44, 47, 48, 49, 52, 53, 54, 55, 56, 61, 62, 64, 65, 66, 68, 69, 70, 72, 73, 81, 85, 86, 87, 89, 90, 92, 93, 95, 96, 98, 100, 109, 132
conservation, 59
Consolidated Appropriations Act, 54
consolidation, 13, 49
construction, vii, 1, 4, 5, 7, 8, 9, 25, 38, 45, 47, 53, 66, 67, 68, 69, 87, 89, 93
consumption, 22, 58
content analysis, 127
controversial, vii, 3, 4, 44
cooling, 37, 56
coordination, 69, 70
cost, vii, 4, 5, 8, 9, 10, 18, 19, 26, 37, 38, 45, 46, 50, 53, 54, 56, 57, 59, 71, 81, 87, 88, 89, 98, 110
cost constraints, 71
cost controls, 110
cost effectiveness, 26, 45
cost-benefit analysis, 88
criminal activity, 21, 24, 71
criminal justice system, 88
criticism, 3, 8
crowding out, 5
current ratio, 110

D

database, 62, 128, 132
debt service, 39
deconcentration, 21, 89
deficiencies, 112, 113, 114, 127
deficit, 98
Department of Health and Human Services, 53
Department of Transportation, 116
destruction, 66
development assistance, 25
dignity, 16
disability, 20, 31, 97
disaster, 132
discrimination, 6
displacement, 83, 91
disposition, 9, 18, 19, 26, 27, 28, 43, 52, 92
distress, 9, 69, 71, 78, 90
distribution, 29, 35
District of Columbia, 76, 127
draft, 15, 44, 108, 125
drugs, 38, 68

E

earnings, 22, 98
economic development, 40, 69, 72, 75
economic growth, vii, 4
education, 79, 82, 91, 101

educational opportunities, 40, 72
educational programs, 26
electricity, 51
emergency, 41, 43
employees, 98
employment, viii, 9, 10, 16, 25, 26, 39, 69, 95, 100
energy, 58, 59, 88
enforcement, viii, 95, 99
environment, 91
equity, 81, 88
ethnicity, 31
evidence, 107, 129
evolution, 51
execution, 86
Executive Order, 132
exercise, viii, 103, 106
expenditures, 26, 37, 80, 109
expertise, 80, 93

F

Fair Housing Act, 17, 21
faith, 85
families, vii, viii, 1, 2, 3, 4, 5, 6, 7, 8, 9, 10, 11, 14, 20, 21, 22, 23, 24, 25, 26, 27, 31, 33, 34, 35, 45, 46, 47, 48, 51, 52, 53, 59, 65, 67, 68, 69, 71, 84, 85, 87, 88, 97, 98, 99, 109, 133
family income, 7, 9, 21, 22, 23, 32
fear, 9
federal assistance, 46
federal funds, 13, 37, 46, 83, 112, 126
federal government, vii, 1, 2, 3, 4, 8, 12, 18, 39, 46, 49, 56, 67, 89, 98
federal law, 12, 15, 21, 22, 126, 132
federal operating subsidies, vii, 9, 55
Federal Register, 25, 50, 52, 54, 60, 63, 64, 74, 77, 78, 100
federal regulations, 12
federal rental housing assistance program, vii, 1
financial, viii, 14, 17, 22, 35, 53, 84, 103, 104, 105, 106, 108, 109, 110, 111, 112, 113, 114, 115, 116, 117, 118, 119, 120, 121, 122, 123, 124, 125, 126, 127, 128, 132
financial condition, 17, 110, 111
financial data, viii, 103, 104, 105, 106, 108, 110, 112, 115, 117, 118, 119, 120, 121, 122, 125, 128
financial resources, 14
flexibility, 26, 52, 132
food, 51, 84
formula, vii, viii, 2, 11, 37, 38, 41, 55, 56, 57, 58, 59, 60, 61, 62, 63, 93, 109
fraud, 17, 113, 117, 121
funding, vii, viii, 2, 3, 7, 8, 9, 10, 11, 16, 17, 24, 25, 26, 27, 37, 38, 39, 40, 41, 42, 43, 46, 47, 49, 50, 52, 53, 54, 55, 57, 58, 59, 61, 63, 65, 69, 70, 71, 73, 74, 75, 76, 78, 80, 81, 83, 85, 86, 88, 89, 90, 91, 96, 113, 114, 126, 133

G

GAO, viii, 50, 80, 82, 84, 85, 89, 90, 92, 93, 103, 104, 105, 106, 114, 120, 122, 125, 127, 132, 133
garbage, 51
General Accounting Office, 80, 81, 92, 93
general expenses, 38
government intervention, 4
governments, 91
grant programs, 109
grants, 2, 10, 12, 37, 38, 39, 40, 41, 43, 66, 72, 74, 75, 76, 77, 78, 79, 85, 90, 91, 92, 93, 100, 109
graph, 35
Great Depression, vii, 4, 45
growth, 45, 68
guidance, 19, 49, 50, 52, 53, 72, 96, 99, 117, 132
guidelines, 33, 52, 53

H

health, 9, 18, 24, 69, 104, 117
HHS, 53

high school, 101
high school diploma, 101
highways, 67
hiring, 25, 87
history, vii, 2, 3, 4, 47, 51, 66, 67, 76, 84, 87, 96
homeowners, 26
homes, 26, 28, 69, 81
HOPE VI, v, viii, 2, 10, 11, 28, 37, 39, 40, 41, 43, 45, 65, 66, 67, 69, 70, 71, 72, 73, 74, 75, 76, 77, 78, 79, 80, 81, 82, 83, 84, 85, 86, 87, 88, 89, 90, 91, 92, 93, 96, 100, 109, 126, 127
hostilities, 6
House, 44, 54, 66, 90, 92, 93, 96, 100
household composition, 23
household income, 22, 82
Housing and Urban Development, viii, 3, 7, 8, 25, 41, 48, 50, 52, 53, 54, 56, 65, 67, 80, 96, 100, 101, 103, 105, 106, 108, 124, 125, 126, 130
housing shortages, 45
HUD financial data, viii, 103, 106, 128

I

illegal drug use, 21, 24
improvements, 38, 69, 70, 82, 86, 91, 123
imputed income, 20
incidence, 69
income, vii, viii, 1, 2, 5, 6, 7, 9, 11, 12, 14, 18, 20, 21, 22, 23, 24, 25, 26, 31, 32, 33, 34, 35, 37, 38, 39, 40, 44, 45, 46, 48, 51, 52, 56, 57, 59, 61, 63, 65, 66, 68, 70, 71, 72, 82, 84, 87, 88, 89, 91, 93, 96, 98, 109, 110, 133
income determination, 12
independent living, 25
individuals, 25, 31, 50
industries, 4
inevitability, 45
inflation, 58
information technology, 59
institutions, 71
interim regulations, 52
internal controls, 113, 114
investment, 3, 37, 38, 91
investments, 37
investors, 89
issues, 2, 3, 4, 42, 67, 81, 89, 104, 108, 113, 115, 116, 121, 123, 124, 125, 127, 128

J

job skills, 100
job training, 25, 26

K

Korea, 6

L

land acquisition, 66
laws, 25, 71, 73, 109, 126, 132
laws and regulations, 25
lead, vii, 4, 13, 44, 49, 91, 93
leadership, 69
legislation, 2, 3, 7, 11, 40, 43, 44, 66, 90
lending, 82
lifetime, 21, 24
light, 43, 44, 46, 115
liquidity, 117, 121
litigation, 27, 93
living conditions, 68, 84
living environment, 5, 71
loans, 11, 39, 44, 83
local government, 4, 12, 13, 39, 66, 67, 72, 75, 91, 109, 131
low-income families, vii, 1, 6, 20, 21, 25, 26, 31, 46, 48, 68, 71, 87, 88, 109, 133
Low-Income Housing Tax Credit, 81
Low-Income Housing Tax Credits (LIHTC), 81
low-rent public housing program, vii, 1, 3, 4, 5, 12, 19, 46

M

majority, 12, 31, 34, 42, 46, 48, 53, 68, 72, 75, 83, 85, 121
management, viii, 6, 10, 14, 16, 17, 20, 28, 38, 39, 43, 52, 55, 56, 59, 60, 61, 64, 67, 70, 72, 85, 105, 108, 110, 111, 112, 113, 114, 115, 116, 117, 119, 121, 122, 123, 126, 128, 129, 132, 133
Maryland, 77, 106, 107, 127, 129
materials, 5, 43
media, 93, 99, 113
median, 9, 21, 32, 35, 48, 51, 53
Medicaid, 88
medical, 22
mentoring, 85
mergers, 13
methodology, 50, 80, 107
metropolitan areas, 51
Miami, 105, 107, 113, 126, 129
middle class, 67
mission, 14, 45
missions, 12
Missouri, 77
misuse, 104, 107, 113, 117, 123
mixed income communities, viii, 65
mixing, 21, 70
models, 2, 3, 7, 8, 45
modernization, 16, 25, 37, 38, 50, 53, 83
modifications, 18
Montana, 77
moratorium, 8, 47, 68
Moses, 93
multifamily rental housing properties, vii, 1

N

natural gas, 51
noncitizens, 20
non-citizens, 20
nonprofit organizations, 109, 118, 131

O

Obama, viii, 13, 40, 44, 49, 65, 66, 90, 91
Obama Administration, viii, 40, 44, 49, 65, 66, 91
Office of Management and Budget, 62, 73, 105, 126, 132
officials, ix, 12, 103, 106, 112, 115, 116, 120, 121, 122, 126, 127, 128, 129
oil, 51
Oklahoma, 77
on-the-job training, 100
operating costs, 56, 58, 61, 63, 68
operations, 4, 14, 16, 37, 110, 111, 113, 116, 117, 119
opportunities, 9, 16, 25, 39, 45, 69, 70, 120, 125
opt out, 132
organize, 16
oversight, viii, 17, 103, 104, 106, 107, 108, 109, 110, 112, 113, 114, 115, 116, 117, 119, 120, 123, 124, 125, 126, 133

P

Pacific, 32
pairing, 8
participants, 7, 14, 25, 45
penalties, 79
per capita income, 82
performers, 17, 49, 112
permission, 18
permit, 44, 109, 125
persons with disabilities, 33, 109
physical characteristics, 39, 72
platform, 48
policy, vii, 2, 3, 5, 6, 8, 12, 16, 19, 20, 22, 34, 42, 43, 45, 46, 51, 52, 98
policy issues, vii, 2, 3, 42
policy making, 19
poor performance, 87
population, 34, 53, 68, 75
portfolio, 58, 106, 123, 128

poverty, 7, 21, 28, 29, 30, 33, 39, 53, 68, 72, 89, 91
President, 5, 8, 44, 47, 49, 53, 68, 90, 96, 104, 105, 107
President Clinton, 96
President Obama, 90
prevention, 15
private investment, 2, 81
privatization, 2, 44
profit, 70, 80, 91, 97
program administration, 16
project, 18, 50, 58, 61, 70, 71, 75, 79, 84, 88, 89, 98
propane, 51
protection, 18
public assistance, 6, 7, 47, 71, 82
public housing authorities (PHAs), vii, 1, 3, 4, 12, 55, 66, 67, 96
public resources, 66
public sector, 100
public service, 71
publicly assisted housing, vii, 1, 88, 100
public-private partnerships, 10
Puerto Rico, 77

Q

quality assurance, 113, 115
quality control, 113
Quality Housing and Work Responsibility Act, viii, 49, 95, 96, 100, 132
quality of life, 3, 16

R

race, 7, 31, 47
reality, 11
recession, 43
recommendations, 9, 15, 58, 69, 70, 104, 106, 108, 110, 114, 118, 125
reconstruction, 70, 71
recovery, 17
redevelopment, 10, 11, 39, 71, 80, 82, 85, 88
reform, 10, 52, 56, 67, 71, 96
Reform, 48, 49, 96, 132
reforms, viii, 55, 81
regulations, vii, 1, 3, 11, 12, 13, 14, 16, 19, 49, 50, 96, 109, 126, 132
rehabilitation, 18, 21, 25, 27, 42, 44, 66, 70, 71, 76, 89
relative size, 29
reliability, 107, 114, 128
rent, vii, 1, 3, 4, 5, 6, 7, 9, 12, 13, 14, 19, 20, 22, 23, 25, 26, 35, 37, 43, 44, 45, 46, 51, 56, 57, 59, 67, 68, 84, 92, 93, 98, 110, 133
repair, 111
reputation, 28
requirements, viii, 4, 5, 14, 15, 26, 34, 40, 48, 50, 51, 55, 59, 70, 78, 79, 84, 89, 96, 97, 98, 99, 106, 107, 110, 113, 114, 116, 132
researchers, 13, 88
reserves, 110
resolution, 92, 110, 116
resources, 9, 11, 39, 43, 69, 70, 72, 76, 79, 80, 83, 109, 111, 116, 122, 125
response, 2, 3, 5, 12, 45, 99, 113, 118
restrictions, 2, 18, 32, 50
retirement, 18
revenue, 59, 88, 110
Revitalization of Distressed Public Housing program, viii, 65
rights, 24
risk, viii, 103, 104, 106, 107, 108, 115, 117, 118, 119, 120, 121, 122, 123, 124, 125, 128, 132, 133
risk factors, 132
rules, vii, 1, 3, 11, 12, 13, 14, 17, 19, 23, 26, 35, 40, 43, 49, 50, 67, 72, 89, 133

S

safety, 10, 15, 18, 24, 37, 38, 63, 69
sanctions, 17, 112
savings, 41, 42, 54, 62, 88
school, 38, 71, 83, 91, 101
scope, 46, 66, 91, 107, 126, 128

security, 10, 16, 37, 38, 43, 63, 70, 111
security guard, 38
segregation, 6
self-sufficiency, viii, 9, 11, 15, 23, 24, 34, 40, 45, 69, 72, 85, 95, 96, 97, 98, 133
Senate, 48, 96, 100, 106
service organizations, 98
services, 14, 24, 37, 38, 40, 45, 66, 69, 70, 71, 72, 76, 79, 85, 91, 101
sewage, 51
sex, 21, 24
shape, vii, 4
shortage, 88, 89
showing, 108, 118, 119, 129
signs, 108, 117, 121
small businesses, 83
small communities, 66, 72, 75
social capital, 45
social ills, 3, 68
Social Security, 33, 99, 100
social services, 10, 16, 69, 83
socialism, 4
South Dakota, 77
sovereignty, 4
spending, 11, 79, 86, 110
SSI, 33
stability, 112
staffing, 37, 93
stakeholder groups, 57
state, 2, 4, 9, 12, 16, 21, 24, 25, 29, 33, 43, 48, 58, 69, 76, 80, 97, 109, 117, 131, 133
state laws, 12
states, 4, 12, 13, 48, 66, 76, 99, 115
stimulus, 2, 11, 40, 43, 53
structure, 7, 11, 45
style, 28
subsidy, 37, 57, 60, 61, 88
Supreme Court, 7, 52
survival, 36

T

target, 9, 31
taxes, 59
technical assistance, 17, 66, 70, 75, 87, 112, 116
technical support, 75
tenants, 3, 5, 6, 7, 18, 21, 22, 24, 35, 37, 44, 51, 56, 57, 59, 67, 68, 75, 84, 97, 98, 99
tenure, 35, 36
testing, 9, 109, 114
theft, 116
tracks, 67
training, 16, 17, 25, 97, 100
transactions, 39, 83, 118
transformation, 91
transformations, 82
transportation, 71, 91
Treasury, 86, 87
treatment, 4

U

unemployment insurance, 88
unemployment rate, 82
unit cost, 43
United, v, 2, 29, 73, 100, 103, 106, 133
United States, v, 2, 29, 73, 100, 103, 106, 133
up-front costs, 88
urban, 7
urban renewal, 7
utility costs, 22, 58

V

vacancies, 63
vandalism, 71
violence, 68
violent crime, 82
vision, 6
Vitter, 100
vocational education, 100
volunteer work, 97, 98
vote, 100
vouchers, 10, 15, 19, 28, 45, 46, 75, 83, 84, 85, 92, 98, 133

W

waiver, 132
war, 5, 7, 46
Washington, 47, 48, 77, 92, 93, 106, 107, 126, 127, 129, 132, 133
waste, 113, 117, 122
water, 51
welfare, 10, 22, 24, 33, 34, 51, 68, 88, 95, 97
welfare reform, 10, 95
well-being, 88
Wisconsin, 77
wood, 51
work activities, 34, 97, 99, 100
workers, 5
working class, 5
working families, 20, 22, 34
World War I, 5, 45